Turning Pragmatism into Practice

Also by this author:

Revisiting Dewey: Best Practices for Educating the Whole Child Today

Turning Pragmatism into Practice

A Vision for Social Studies Teachers

Daniel W. Stuckart

ROWMAN & LITTLEFIELD
Lanham • Boulder • New York • London

Published by Rowman & Littlefield
A wholly owned subsidiary of The Rowman & Littlefield Publishing Group, Inc.
4501 Forbes Boulevard, Suite 200, Lanham, Maryland 20706
www.rowman.com

Unit A, Whitacre Mews, 26–34 Stannary Street, London SE11 4AB

Copyright © 2018 by Daniel W. Stuckart

All rights reserved. No part of this book may be reproduced in any form or by any electronic or mechanical means, including information storage and retrieval systems, without written permission from the publisher, except by a reviewer who may quote passages in a review.

British Library Cataloguing-in-Publication Information Available

Library of Congress Cataloging-in-Publication Data Available
ISBN: 978-1-4758-3770-4 (cloth : alk. paper)
ISBN: 978-1-4758-3771-1 (pbk. : alk. paper)
ISBN: 978-1-4758-3772-8 (electronic)

∞™ The paper used in this publication meets the minimum requirements of American National Standard for Information Sciences—Permanence of Paper for Printed Library Materials, ANSI/NISO Z39.48–1992.

Printed in the United States of America

Contents

List of Tables	vii
List of Figure	ix
Foreword	xi
Preface	xv
Acknowledgments	xix
Introduction	1
Suggested Text Engagement 2	
A Note about Dewey's Major Works 3	
1 Nature	5
From Humble Origins to Greatness 7	
His Works 8	
Dewey and the Social Studies 9	
A Radical Turn in Philosophy 12	
The Social Studies Wars Revisited 17	
Developing a Democratic Vision for Teaching Social Studies 21	
Summary 26	
2 Curriculum	27
The Sources of School Subject Matter 29	
The Social Studies Teacher's Interaction 33	
The Three Pedagogical Traditions 37	
Designing and Implementing a Reflective Inquiry Curriculum 41	

    The Social Studies Curriculum Continuum 49
    Summary 51

3 Experience   53
    Experience and the Natural World 54
    Dewey, Experience, and Education 59
    Experience and Judgment 64
    History Education as Instrumental 68
    Summary 70

4 Morality   71
    Interest and Effort 73
    Valuation and Ethics 79
    Moral Philosophy 83
    Summary 88

5 Inquiry   90
    A Return to Dewey's Ontology 91
    Doing the Social Studies 98
    The Curious Case of the Common Core State Standards 103
    Summary 105

6 Citizenship   107
    Dewey's Democracy 108
    The Social Studies 115
    Summary 121

References   123

Index   133

About the Author   137

List of Tables

0.1	Crafting a Social Studies Teacher Vision	2
0.2	John Dewey's Major Works with Original Publication Dates	3
1.1	Using Deweyan Philosophy to Construct a Social Studies Teacher Rationale	25
2.1	Characteristics, Pros, and Cons of Curriculum Structures to Support a Deweyan Approach to Learning Social Studies	44
2.2	The Social Studies Curriculum Continuum	48

List of Figure

3.1 The Phases of Experience   56

Foreword

Unfortunately, becoming a social studies teacher resembles both an endurance race and entering a hall of mirrors. In most teacher education programs students will be asked to show they can plan lessons that draw from the gamut of the social science disciplines found on university campuses. They will learn that there is no consensus among university professors about what social studies is.

They will be taught to prioritize the teaching of disciplinary concepts and methods, as well as the assessment of students' ability to apply these concepts to real-world problems. They will be told that they must attend to depth over breadth. They will be asked to plan lessons that adhere to the guidelines of local school districts. They will not be asked to reflect upon how the guidelines align with educational principles they were taught.

While teaching students, they will be required to follow a curriculum that has been ratified by school administrators. This pattern will emphasize teaching breadth over depth. To attain certification, they will have to teach three to five lessons that are focused on a given theme. They will discover that cooperating teachers rarely devote three to five lessons on a given theme because they have too much information they have to cover.

They will notice that secondary students don't really see much connection between the content of their social studies classes and the worlds they know. They will also notice that secondary students don't like social studies. When completing the program they will be asked to write a reflection explaining how the program helped to prepare them to be a high quality teacher.

Becoming a high quality social studies teacher requires years of thoughtful practice while, over time, addressing the controversies alluded to above. Of central importance is for the teacher to develop a mature rationale of the significance and scope of the social studies for her or him. Indeed, it is a commonplace in educational circles that a teacher ought to plan curriculum with an idea in mind of what the ultimate goals of a content area are.

Throughout the history of the field of social studies there has been a great deal of tension between the perceived imperative to teach the social science disciplines, a general requirement we have seen of contemporary social studies programs, and the idea that students, as citizens of a democracy, need to be introduced to fulfilling that role in schools.

This tension can be seen in the following quotation taken from the 1916 *Report on Social Studies,* written by the Committee on Social Studies of the Commission on the Reorganization of Secondary Education of the National Education Association. This document articulates the founding animus of the field of social studies:

> From the standpoint of the purposes of secondary education, it is far less important that the adolescent youth should acquire a comprehensive knowledge of any or all of the social sciences than it is that he *[sic]* should be given experience and practice in the observation of social phenomena as he encounters them; that he should be brought to understand that every social problem is many-sided and complex; and that he should acquire the habit of dispassionate consideration of all the facts available. This, the committee believes, can best be accomplished by dealing with actual situations as they occur, and by drafting into service the materials of all of the social sciences as occasion demands for a thorough understanding of the situation in question.

While the committee was clearly on the side of introducing students to the practice of being a citizen of a democracy, it can be seen that they also valued the role of the social sciences in addressing contemporary social problems. Orchestrating a synthesis of appropriate concepts to address real-world problems and to do so in a way that will successfully engage students requires a level of the teacher's professional capacity that is not usually recognized.

This book will help a beginning and mature teacher address the rigors of curriculum development and teaching in social studies by providing a vision of the proper scope of social studies grounded in the work of John Dewey. It is not surprising that Dewey's philosophy is useful in this regard.

Although he was not a member of the committee that crafted the 1916 guidelines for social studies, many scholars have pointed to his influence on the committee as well as the phenomena of the committee's and Dewey's shared recognition of the problems of how to intellectually prepare citizens for an urban, industrial and modernizing world. Indeed, we are still facing these same questions today.

Professor Stuckart has undertaken the extremely important task of elaborating specific concepts Dewey developed in his philosophy that address problems that continue to occur with social studies as it is commonly taught.

Among the key challenges of teaching social studies that he addresses with the help of John Dewey are the relationship between social science concepts and the world they were developed to address, the fluid and evolving nature of social science concepts, the need to help students see the meaningfulness of concepts, the need for students to organize their studies around inquiries pertaining to persistent social issues, and the need for students to establish democratic norms of shared discovery in classrooms.

It is quite rare for an author to confront the challenge of making difficult philosophical ideas relevant for acting in the world as it is. Indeed, one suspects that the intellectual work that Professor Stuckart offers here is a prerequisite for any sustained reform of the challenges that persist in the teaching of social studies. This text should provide intellectual guidance and justification for all social studies teachers who wish to address many of the issues that have bedeviled the field since its inception.

John Hunter Gunn, retired, Department of Secondary Education and Youth Services, Queens College, City University of New York

Preface

I began thinking about this book nearly six years ago after I coauthored another about Dewey's philosophy of educating the whole child. At the time, I asked myself, "Why hasn't the social studies scholarly community written more to ground the discipline in Dewey's system of ideas?" It seemed to me that much of the Dewey scholarship in the field emphasized the historical deliberations leading to the 1916 report of the Committee on Social Studies and how the founders of the curriculum turned to Dewey for inspiration and the ideas to experiment with a curriculum that rode the progressive wave of being attentive to students' needs and interests while providing the conditions for social-issues inquiry.

In the ensuing years, some scholars questioned Dewey's commitment to his interdisciplinary problem-solving model as a paradox, citing his discussion of individual disciplines in works such as *Democracy and Education* (1916). However, they missed the mark because the real paradox was Dewey's insistence that individuality requires community. No individual can flourish beyond an elaborated social network. Attending to the health of this network requires that citizens keep a careful eye on democracy, including investigations into social problems and the judicious deliberation of solutions that benefit the most people.

The newly minted social studies curriculum articulated a citizenship model founded on Deweyan principles where students did not merely learn disciplinary knowledge like history and civics, but were to learn it *in the service* of studying and addressing those problems. The dilemma, though, was that the guidelines also privileged disciplinary knowledge, which has created confusion and fueled the cultural wars over the teaching of history ever since.

The privileging of disciplinary forms of knowledge was a committee compromise that has resulted in several intended and unintended consequences.

First, the main professional organization, the National Council for the Social Studies (NCSS) founded in 1921, has issued a dizzying array of standards, best practices, and position statements trying to be everything to most people. The most generous interpretation means that teachers are disproportionately utilizing valuable instructional time for disciplinary concepts at the expense of inquiry and social issue investigations.

Second, there has never been a comprehensive explanation of *why* Dewey's system is the appropriate way to learn these disciplines. A big part of the problem is that the field's teacher educators have never agreed upon what those ideas are and how they should work. Dewey's entire philosophical system can be defined by a rejection of fixed ends. Fixed ends imply that you learn something for no other reason than as an end in itself, which is what the social studies contrarians have been arguing about the study of history for over the past century. And perhaps more importantly, it means that whatever that something is, it remains unchanged and can never be diminished or improved.

Third, a rejection of fixed ends and Dewey's emphasis on the changing aspects of living meant that he created a system that dissolved the dualism trap that had plagued philosophy at least since the ancient Greeks forcing philosophers to argue things like the mind could come to know something independent of the body. Humans interact with other beings and the environment using their entire psychical and physical selves, which Dewey encapsulated in his concept of *an* experience. In sum, he argued that these interactions constituted reality, and there could be no objective reality beyond human agency.

And lastly, many scholars have written about Dewey either thematically or piecemeal—through the lens of democracy, inquiry, dispositions, and other topics—exceedingly well. However, to my knowledge, nobody has ever connected all the dots and presented a comprehensive version of his philosophical system. Why should we be surprised then that the social studies field is so atomized when the philosophical and intellectual bearings are as well? One of the subthemes I explore throughout the book is why Dewey is so often misunderstood, including the notion that he bears some of the responsibility for this state of affairs.

What is a social studies teacher to do—especially considering all the state and local standards and a testing regime that favors memorization? I found one exemplar in an unlikely place. I recently attended a meeting at a District 79 high school in New York City. District 79 is an alternative designation for schools and programs serving students with interrupted studies. In a chance encounter with a social studies teacher at the school, I struck up a conversation and realized that the school environment was ideal for a social studies approach to learning—quite the opposite of most traditional schools where disciplinary teaching flourishes because of the all-consuming focus of teaching to the New York State Regents exams.

As the teacher explained to me, most of her students were recent immigrants and she had to design daily lessons with the assumption that she would encounter a completely new group of students. The students attended school sporadically because they moved often and worked long hours to help support their families. In other words, they did not have the luxury of attending school consistently because their lives were hardscrabble and precarious.

Consequently, the teacher constructed lessons around themes and investigations of interest to the students. She spent the beginning of every period talking with the class and then strategically interacting with individual members to direct them to appropriate curricular resources. They often worked in small groups as they learned history through the study of social problems salient to their lives engaging with topics such as immigration, human rights, and economic opportunity.

The teacher was not sure about her overall impact, though, because a typical semester ended with only one or two students from her original class list. Despite the fluid attendance, the teacher hewed to Dewey's position that a skill-based approach facilitated a continuity of learner experience and that knowledge was a reconstruction of that experience.

In the final analysis, Dewey's system is a middle position that accommodates both the fixed (i.e., content) and changing (i.e., skills) aspects of the curriculum. Simply put, in experience a learner needs both because skills allow one to test truth claims while incorporating the facts and concepts of content as evidence. The hope is that my modest contribution will help illuminate the way for a more interactive curriculum faithful to its origins in Dewey's philosophy.

Daniel W. Stuckart, Lehman College,
City University of New York, September 2017

Acknowledgments

I am deeply grateful to Drs. Stephen Thornton, John Gunn, Thomas Misco, and Kenneth Carano for their willingness to read the manuscript and offer sage advice. With their contributions, my hope is that this book will both fill a void in the scholarly literature and offer a neglected tool to social studies teachers and teacher candidates for achieving a vision of an interactive curriculum.

Introduction

The purpose of this book is to guide teachers and teacher candidates in developing, implementing, and reflecting on a vision for an interactive social studies curriculum. The book is organized into six chapters representing major theoretical concepts from John Dewey's philosophy, a version of pragmatism that he later called instrumentalism, which the founders of the modern social studies movement adopted in their grand curriculum experiment nearly a century ago.

The reader should think of the chapter arrangement as a progressive journey to demystify the purpose and use of the social studies curriculum beyond the dictates of standards. Instead, Dewey's philosophy and theories provide tools for engaging with the curriculum. The engagement results in a transaction among students, the teacher, and the environment, where in the end, all are changed. The scope of the book begins with the first chapter exploring the co-emergence of Dewey's ideas and the social studies movement; and ends in chapter 6 with his radical proposition for democracy and citizenship.

The middle chapters explain Dewey's minimum unit of analysis and how it functions in existence. Chapters 2 and 3, curriculum and experience respectively, represent his central focus because the former includes other people's experiences and the latter is about how individuals transact with the environment. Dewey unapologetically elevated the individual above all else in his system of ideas as he explicated how curriculum could be used in experience to make sense of the world. Curriculum and experience, moreover, are merely names for history.

Next, in chapter 4, a key concern for Dewey was ethics, and hence, the discussion turns to the conditions for a moral life as one considers the consequences of her or his actions on others, including the proper role of interest and effort. Because the social studies teacher also transacts with the classroom environment, she or he has an obligation to engage in reflective activity, as well as provide students opportunities for character education.

Chapter 5 reveals how inquiry allows individuals to transcend problematic situations using intelligence to survive, thrive, and achieve satisfaction, which is why a powerful social studies curriculum ought to present situations for students to identify social problems, deliberate solutions, exercise judgments, and form beliefs that are always tentative and subject to further revision. During inquiry, students reconstruct their experiences in the foreground of a dynamic, problematic society.

SUGGESTED TEXT ENGAGEMENT

One of the themes investigated throughout this book is that even though Dewey's ideas are central to the social studies curriculum, most educators never develop a depth of understanding, which provides the grist for best practices. The main reason may be that Dewey's writings are dense, his style stilted, and only against the backdrop of seven decades of prolific scholarship can readers develop a coherent whole. This book is an attempt to short-circuit that process, which fittingly is also Dewey's goal for modern education.

Therefore, the recommendation is to use table 0.1 as a planning document. As you proceed through the book, pause often to reflect on how your preconceived notions differ and perhaps change throughout your engagement with the text. Think about your interpretation and what it means for teaching.

Table 0.1. Crafting a Social Studies Teacher Vision

Chapters	Vision Elements	Your Planning Notes
1. Nature	• Construct a social studies rationale incorporating Deweyan principles: 　◦ Accessibility 　◦ Being continuous with the natural world 　◦ Experience as the minimum unit of analysis 　◦ Democracy as an ethical/moral ideal 　◦ Purpose/reform of schools	
2. Curriculum	• Analyze your beliefs about purpose and aim of social studies • Commit to implementing more than a linear, chronological history curriculum by incorporating activities such as: 　◦ Long-term projects 　◦ Thematic units 　◦ Issues-centered units/lessons 　◦ Reverse chronology units	

Chapters	Vision Elements	Your Planning Notes
3. Experience	• Identify the experiences the students bring to school and bridge the gap between them and the curriculum to promote instrumental, cognitive activity	
4. Morality	• Assist students in identifying and developing their interests • Evaluate your character traits and attitudes after every activity considering wider consequences to change your conduct • Integrate opportunities for students to engage in reflective moral activities	
5. Inquiry	• Make an inquiry curriculum where students frequently engage with contemporary social problems, and then consider possibilities and consequences leading to action	
6. Citizenship	• Refine your rationale with CPI and local values • Learn to conduct many different types of discussion strategies • Provide multimodal opportunities for students to take social action within and outside the curriculum • Contribute to a school-wide democratic culture	

Table 0.2. John Dewey's Major Works with Original Publication Dates

SS	*The School and Society* (1899)	EN	*Experience and Nature* (1929)
CC	*The Child and the Curriculum* (1902)	TML	*Theory of the Moral Life* (1932)
HWT	*How We Think* (1910)	AE	*Art as Experience* (1934)
IEE	*Interest and Effort in Education* (1913)	EE	*Experience and Education* (1938)
DE	*Democracy and Education* (1916)	LTI	*Logic: The Theory of Inquiry* (1938)
RP	*Reconstruction in Philosophy* (1920)	TV	*Theory of Valuation* (1939)
PIP	*The Public and Its Problems* (1927)		

A NOTE ABOUT DEWEY'S MAJOR WORKS

Given the volume and complexity of Dewey's works, the major texts are abbreviated in the citations. For example, a standard Dewey quotation citation from *Democracy and Education* appears like this (*DE*, p. 201) rather than (Dewey, 1916/2007, p. 201). All the works are philosophical, but some contain major educational significance as shown in table 0.2 with the original publication dates.

Further, as you read please notice how the arguments return to Dewey's later writings, also known as his naturalistic phase as he returns to a logic based on Darwinian evolution and change. These specific works represent the wisdom of an extraordinary philosopher, psychologist, and sociologist who not only provided the intellectual impetus for the social studies curriculum, but also influenced the shape and direction of modern education like no person ever before or since.

Chapter 1

Nature

Focus Questions:

1 What are the connections between John Dewey and the origins of the modern social studies curriculum?
2 What are the characteristics of Dewey's theory of nature?
3 In what ways does Dewey's instrumentalism inform a vision for teaching social studies?

Compared to other school subjects, the social studies is a young curriculum emerging in the late nineteenth century during a fertile period in educational theory and philosophy. Science, discovery, revolution and an unleashing of social forces transformed Enlightenment ideals into rich philosophical systems such as transcendentalism, Marxism, positivism, and many others. By the turn of the century, one particularly influential philosophy, pragmatism, became a major force in the curriculum reform movements of the early twentieth century.

Although the term pragmatism first appeared in print around the end of the nineteenth century, the foundations stretch back to the 1870s. The pioneers included William James, Charles Sanders Peirce, George Herbert Mead, Chauncey Wright, and John Dewey. It was Dewey though, who developed a robust system of ideas based on his unique construction of pragmatism, which he later called "Instrumentalism" (Dewey, 1984, p. 3).

When the Committee on Social Studies (CSS) issued their final report in 1916, Dewey's ideas permeated the recommendations even though he was not involved with any of the proceedings. As Nelson (1994) noted, "Dewey and the scientific approach to curriculum and schooling were favorably viewed by most of the school people on the Committee" (p. 75). Like pragmatism, the antecedents of the social studies occurred much earlier.

Pragmatism and the social studies followed similar trajectories because both were reactions to the great social upheavals of the Industrial Revolution. The foundation of the social studies originated in the social welfare movements of the 1880s. Later, the sociology-inspired curricula of the 1910s informed the deliberations of the CSS, which by the end of the 1930s, culminated in a formal social studies subject matter.

In fact, Saxe (1992) concluded, "Clearly, no part of the school curriculum (past or present) appeared as close to Deweyan thought as social studies" (p. 266). Similarly, Fallace (2009) revealed that during the deliberations, the CSS embraced two central tenets of Deweyan philosophy in order to bridge vast ideological differences among competing factions: the addressing of present problems or needs and the development of aims for improving society. In other words, the committee's final report was a compromise or middle position based on an interpretation of Dewey's works.

The origin of the social studies curriculum represented Deweyan thought in action where his ideas functioned as the *method* for bridging differences among competing factions and as the *content* for addressing present problems and needs. Because Dewey only offered two public remarks about the social studies curriculum—and his support appeared ambiguous at best—some academics concluded that a paradox formed between his interdisciplinary approach to problem solving and his focus on traditional, stand-alone social sciences like geography and history in some of his major works (Fallace, 2009; Saxe, 1992; Stanley & Stanley III, 1977).

This chapter begins with an explanation of how Dewey's instrumentalism represents a radical departure from classical philosophy and how the founders of the modern social studies fashioned the new curriculum with Dewey as the ideological center. Next, the discussion shows how his philosophy incorporates nineteenth century ideas derived from the new theory of evolution—a theory of nature—where content and method become unified in a person's experiences.

The focus then returns to the social studies arguing that Dewey's middle position respects both the formal canons of knowledge and the process of studying social issues. Further, because theorists and teacher educators broadly misunderstand Dewey's philosophy, as well as his direct and indirect contributions to the field, many teachers lack a vision for effective social studies instruction anchored in a philosophy of democratic deliberation and discourse.

The central problem of the social studies, then, is that too many teachers approach the subject matter from a disciplinary position rather than an inquiry-based, interdisciplinary perspective. In practice, the emphasis on teaching disciplinary concepts often leaves little time and energy for students to engage in inquiry-based and interdisciplinary learning.

Teachers lose sight of the purpose of the social studies as grounded in the development of democratic ideals and dispositions in the citizenry. *A vision for social studies teachers begins with the development of a rationale entrenched in democratic values and attuned to the needs of preparing students to address contemporary social problems. In sum, Dewey offers social studies teachers a rich philosophical and theoretical system for envisioning a dynamic curriculum, something the field has yet to realize in a widespread way.*

FROM HUMBLE ORIGINS TO GREATNESS

Born into a religiously conservative family on October 20, 1859, in Burlington, Vermont, John Dewey rose to prominence as a philosopher and professor whose deep intellect helped fashion the fields of education, psychology, and sociology. Although his forbears were farmers, his father broke tradition and opened a small grocery store in Burlington where the young Dewey experienced firsthand the effects of the Industrial Revolution, as well as a cauldron of novel ideas.

Dewey's birth year coincided with the publication of some of the greatest canonical works of Western intellectual history such as Karl Marx's *Critique of Political Economy*, John Stuart Mill's *On Liberty*, and perhaps what would become the most influential on the young Dewey, Charles Darwin's *Origin of Species*. Dewey deftly drew on these works and many others displaying an encyclopedic knowledge of history and philosophy to formulate his own version of pragmatism.

Coming of age in a quintessentially small New England city exposed Dewey to many of the social displacements brought on by the Industrial Revolution, and allowed him to forge friendships with others coming from different social and ethnic backgrounds, which may have instilled a democratic spirit during his youth. This spirit would become the guiding force throughout his long life manifesting in his democratic philosophy, as well as a highly productive academic career.

Dewey established himself as a capable high school student, and at the age of fifteen he matriculated at the University of Vermont where innovative faculty exposed him to emerging, radical philosophical ideas that would nudge him toward a career as a philosopher. Shortly after graduating, he completed a couple of stints as a secondary teacher before eventually studying philosophy at Johns Hopkins University where he earned a doctorate in 1884.

Upon receiving his degree, Dewey moved to the Midwest where he would spend the next twenty years as a faculty member at the University of Michigan (1884–1888) and later at Minnesota (1888–1894) and Chicago (1894–1904).

At the University of Chicago in 1896, he established the Laboratory School where he could experiment with a child-centered curriculum and pedagogy based on research and trial-and-error.

The first textual fruit of these experimental education endeavors commenced with the publication of the *School and Society* in 1899, his first book explicitly directed at school reform, followed by *The Child and the Curriculum* (1902), *How We Think* (1910), and *Democracy and Education* (1916). In 1904 Dewey moved back to the East Coast accepting a dual appointment as a philosophy professor at Columbia University and Teachers College where he taught until his retirement twenty-six years later. He continued to publish after his retirement from Columbia right up until his death in 1952.

With a rising reputation in the twentieth century, he published prolifically about metaphysics, psychology, and education issues, while at the same time, contributing significant insights into contemporary topics like immigration, World War I, politics, and the economy. Although he retired from active teaching in 1930, he continued to write and remained a liberal activist until his death on June 1, 1952, at ninety-two years of age (Dykhuizen, 1959; Westbrook, 1991).

HIS WORKS

While Dewey spent many of his later years explaining, clarifying, and defending his positions, the scope of his work was deep and broad. Astonishingly, his publications exceeded 1,000 items including about 40 books, 140 journal articles, various essays, and numerous speeches. The Dewey compendium is a living embodiment of his philosophy.

In over seventy-one years of intense scholarship, he articulated philosophical and societal problems, considered solutions, and then tested his ideas in experience. By 1890, he had formulated the lifelong foundation for his philosophical principles, but he continued to evolve in scope and detail.

After a thirty-year effort begun in 1961, The Center for Dewey Studies published *The Collected Works of John Dewey* in 1991. Although the editors constructed the series in three volumes, which they called *The Early, Middle,* and *Later Years* and roughly covered twenty to twenty-five years each, they delineated his work chronologically, rather than thematically because of the complexity of his thought (Boydston, 1992/1993).

Organizational Strategies Related to Dewey's Writings

Given the magnitude of the compendium—and perhaps one of many reasons Dewey is often misunderstood—scholars must develop a strategy for selecting appropriate sources in context of his thought that "is neither too narrow nor too broad" (Boisvert, 1988, p. 15). Over the years, writers adopted different approaches including dividing Dewey's life into four periods based on his early years, time as a graduate student, academic appointments in the Midwest, and last years at Columbia and post-retirement (Dykhuizen, 1959). Although these were formative periods for Dewey's biography, they do not capture the intellectual genesis of his thought.

Another approach emphasized a productive thirty-plus-year period spanning his time at the University of Chicago and Columbia University (1894–1930) when Dewey produced his major ideas on education ranging from "My Pedagogic Creed" in 1897 to *Logic: The Theory of Inquiry* in 1938 (Pring, 2007). And yet another partitioned Dewey's works into three phases of about twenty years each: the *idealistic* phase (1882–1903), the *experimental* phase (1904–1924), and the *naturalistic* phase (1925–1953), including the posthumous publication of works in the year after his death (Boisvert, 1988).

Intellectual Trends and Major Works

Because the central focus of this book is about developing a philosophical and theoretical framework for the social studies—not a biography or chronology of events—Boisvert's phases provide a useful guide for thinking about intellectual changes over time, especially Dewey's experimental and naturalistic phases, corresponding roughly from 1900 to 1953. During this period, Dewey cast his early curriculum experiments in the Laboratory School at the University of Chicago against the backdrop of his expansive philosophy yielding valuable insights into social studies concepts and purposes.

In the latter half, he elaborated details of his philosophy and theories in the context of human evolution and existence—the most neglected sources for understanding the importance of education, in general, and especially the social studies discipline! While the early twentieth-century founders of the social studies debated and formulated a new curriculum based on Dewey's principles, they fell short of the mark by failing to recognize the possibilities afforded by his perspective about the evolutionary nature of human relations.

DEWEY AND THE SOCIAL STUDIES

Despite the clear connections between Dewey's system of ideas and the nascent social studies curriculum, Dewey never offered a full, public endorsement of the social studies before, during, or after the founding deliberations. Keeping in mind that he lived over thirty-five years after the 1916 Committee on Social Studies report, he appears to have only commented publicly about social studies twice in that long period. Further, at first glance, his remarks seem ambivalent about supporting the subject matter.

In the first public record, he mentioned social studies while offering tribute to the centennial of Horace Mann's groundbreaking work in Massachusetts in a speech titled, "The Challenge of Democracy to Education," before the Eastern States Regional Conference of the Progressive Education Association in November 1936 when the world was in the throes of the Great Depression. Dewey's main message was that schools must reform to sustain and nurture democracy especially in such trying times when communism and fascism were gaining momentum overseas.

Specifically, changes in school relationships—including methods, subject matter arrangements, and connections to the wider society—were necessary for students to study social problems, and then act on them. As an example of this modern way of thinking, he pointed out the emergence of the social studies:

> It certainly seems as if the social studies have a more intimate relation with social life than a great many of the other subjects that are taught in the school, and that accordingly their increasing introduction into the curriculum, the increasing emphasis upon them ought to be a means by which the school system meets the challenge of democracy.
>
> But the crucial question is the extent to which the material of the social studies, whether economics or politics or history or sociology, whatever it may be, is taught simply as information about present society or is taught in connection with things that are done, that need to be done, and how to do them. If the first tendency prevails, I can readily imagine that the introduction of more and more social studies into the curriculum will simply put one more load onto a curriculum that is already overburdened, and that the supposed end for which they were introduced—the development of a more intelligent citizenship in all the ranges of citizenship (the complex ranges that now exist, including political but including also much more) will be missed. (Dewey, 2008, p. 185)

About sixteen months after the speech, the May 1938 issue of *Progressive Education* featured a Dewey submission, "What is social study?" He began the article with questions about the range of *the* social in the new subject matter, as well as the social nature of *all* subject matter. He concluded with:

> The problem of congestion of studies and diversion of aims with resulting superficiality is a pressing one today.... In the end emphasis upon social studies as a separate line of study may only add to the confusion and dispersion that now exist! Not because they are not important, but precisely because they are so important that they should give direction and organization to all branches of study.
>
> In conclusion.... Social studies as an isolated affair are likely to become either accumulations of bodies of special factual information or, in the hands of

zealous teachers, to be organs of indoctrination in the sense of propaganda for a special social end, accepted enthusiastically, perhaps, but still dogmatically. (Dewey, 1946, p. 183)

What are we to make of these seemingly conflicting attitudes about the social studies discipline where on the one hand, he praises the potential to address social challenges, and on the other, warns that the new field is contributing to an overburdened school curriculum, and worse, has the potential to indoctrinate students?

Dewey neither condemned nor fully supported the relatively new curriculum. Notwithstanding his insistence on connecting all school subjects with the study of social issues, he cautioned schools not to overload an already abundant curriculum with information, and in addition, opined that the isolation of social science concepts from the study of current social issues would allow for indoctrination rather than critical reflection on social problems.

None of these interpretations, though, are satisfactory for answering the question, "Given the apparently close alignment of the new field of social studies with his system of ideas, why did Dewey avoid direct engagement?" This question is particularly salient given his devotion to education over his remaining years.

A Paradox or Misunderstanding?

One of Dewey's most iconic works, *Democracy and Education* (1916), appeared shortly after the CSS's final report where he devoted entire sections to history and geography, much to the consternation of the social studies proponents. One possible explanation is that Dewey was more of a traditionalist who supported stand-alone social sciences and history (Fallace, 2009; Saxe, 1992).

Democracy and Education (1916) offers a "more radical [approach than the CSS final report] in its emphasis on education as a democratic process rather than a prescription of specific content" (Fallace, 2009, p. 618). In a similar vein, one of the few Deweyan analyses of the social studies curriculum suggests that Dewey's focus on the social sciences presents a paradox (Stanley & Stanley III, 1977).

Reconciling Dewey's *interdisciplinary* inquiry approach in problem solving with his emphases on *stand-alone* history and geography subjects, Stanley and Stanley III (1977) argue, "The resolution of this paradox must be sought in the total philosophy of John Dewey" (p. 365). Curiously though, social studies educators never heed this advice in a systematic way.

Most social studies scholarship nibbles on the edges of Deweyan thought and comes in four general varieties: (1) one or a few Deweyan ideas as part of a literature review or to support an academic assertion as in the following example where the only reference to Dewey is made here:

> Specifically, leveraging historical thinking skills, such as recognizing multiple perspectives; developing reasoned judgments of historical causality, consequence and significance; and facilitating modes of documentary inquiry will yield Dewey's vision of Democracy as more than a form of government, but of "a mode of associated living, of conjoint communicated experience." (Swan & Hicks, 2006, p. 144)

(2) Dewey's ideas and the origins of the social studies (e.g., Evans, 2004; Fallace, 2009; Lybarger, 1983; Saxe, 1992); (3) interpretation and analyses through a partial Deweyan lens (e.g., Misco & Shively, 2010; Shaver, 1977; Sherman, 1977; Stanley, 2010; Vinson, 1999; Wheeler, 1977); and finally (4) those that offer extensive Deweyan analysis (e.g., Barr, Barth, & Shermis, 1978; Parker, 2003; Stanley & Stanley III, 1977; Taba, 1967; Thornton, 2005).

In the social studies, Dewey is everywhere, and at the same time, nowhere because the social studies community of scholars has not yet developed a consensus view on the significance of his thought for the social studies. Consequently, most teachers remain unaware of his profound contributions and the potential of his teachings to advance their practices.

A RADICAL TURN IN PHILOSOPHY

Philosophy and science have always engaged in a mutually beneficial relationship. Before the Renaissance, science was philosophy and vice versa. During the Scientific Revolution of the sixteenth and seventeenth centuries, they diverged, but continued to engage in a manner where one informed the other. These events provided the context for John Dewey, especially Darwin's theory of evolution.

Dewey's philosophy emerged *because* of evolution, natural selection, and what he perceived as philosophy's role in addressing scientific progress. Darwin conclusively evinced that individuals adapted to their environments, and over time, natural selection extinguished and favored certain traits within species. Dewey reframed philosophy based on these major scientific discoveries. He developed a metaphysics—a conceptual framework for existence—based on "*experience, interaction,* and *possibility*" (Boisvert, 1988, p. 204).

In keeping with Darwin, his entire paradigm rested on the assumption that any being is continuous with nature. At least five elements suggest his ideas were a radical departure from philosophy in a traditional sense: (1) accessibility; (2) being as continuous with the natural world; (3) experience as the minimum unit of analysis; (4) democracy as an ethical and moral ideal; and (5) the purpose of schools.

Accessibility. The pragmatists—and especially Dewey's instrumentalism—liberated philosophy from the rarefied world of philosophers and placed it in the hands of the masses. While philosophy's concern has always been to delve into the fundamental nature of knowledge, reality, and existence, Dewey insisted that it serve as a tool in human experience to solve everyday problems.

Therefore, Dewey's method in the widest sense possible is a tool for studying, criticizing, and reconsidering a perceived problem. While never being the source of an answer, it is a way of casting a wider net, examining the issue over a longer vista or contextualizing it within an overarching phenomenon, and then evaluating the consequences.

Being as continuous with the natural world. In an evolutionary way, anything that exists adapts in a changing environment, but on all levels, the rates of changes differ (e.g., think about changes within a being and changes between the being and the environment including other beings). Dewey characterized existence as an ebb and flow operation, or in metaphysical terms as a process of form and change where stability, ideal matter, and permanence establish an equal partnership with change, movement, and adaptation.

Experience as the minimum unit of analysis. Human beings engage in one long series of continuous experiences or interactions with the world. Most of the time, individuals experience the world in a primitive way, meaning non-cognitively, and rely on habit to navigate most situations. However, when presented with a problem, the individual can have *an* experience, which is cognitive and contains a beginning, middle, and end. In this scenario, history is an important component of intelligent activity for evaluating future consequences based on current conditions and prior experiences.

Democracy as an ethical and moral ideal. While Dewey clearly elevated the individual above all else, a person has a moral and ethical obligation to contribute to the social realm, and consider the concerns and perspectives of other people. In other words, the ideal social system is a form of democracy where all individuals have the resources and opportunities to flourish in her or his unique way. Moreover, everyone has a moral responsibility to nurture and enhance democracy so others have the chance to flourish as well. The key to this system is communication.

Deweyan democracy is about leveling the opportunity playing field. Every individual has the potential for growth, which conceptually is the same as individual freedom and self-realization. Because every individual is unique, she requires varying types and degrees of resources to reach her potential. All participation is voluntary, but achieving one's potential also benefits others who encounter her in social transactions.

As Westbrook (1991) summarized, "Moral democracy called not only for the pursuit of worthwhile ends but for the pursuit of these ends in ways that enlisted the freely cooperative participation of all concerned" (p. 165). Despite offering a radical, broad interpretation of democracy, Dewey's primary focus was always on the individual and how a democratic community enriched an individual's experience (Cremin, 1959).

School reform. Dewey conceived of schools as an extension of the home. In a modern and complex world, our ancestors developed schools to supplement the traditional family and tribal roles for socializing young people. He placed great faith in schools as a universal institution that prepared youth for community life; as such, schools must be reformed to consider young people's interests, emphasize manual and practical activities, and to use the curriculum to develop students' ability to act *intelligently* in the world, especially through experimentation.

Within the frame of experience, Dewey dissolved the philosophical dualisms such as content and method; theory and practice; knowledge and skills approaches. The old dualisms become unified in an experience. Reflected in this radical departure from traditional philosophy is the fact that Dewey managed to conceive and transmit a vast, coherent metaphysical system rivaling the scope of Aristotle's over 2,000 years earlier.

Greek and Early Modern Metaphysics

One constant throughout human history is that our ancestors developed conceptual tools to address perceived cultural and societal needs. The ancient Greeks were the first civilization to engage in orderly scientific investigations into the natural world, which also meant that they established philosophical terminology like metaphysics, ontology, and epistemology that we still employ today. However, because the original contexts evolved, so too did the meanings of these terms over time.

About three centuries after Aristotle's death, an editor assembling his works coined the term, "metaphysics" or "the things after the physics," but the term did not take on a transcendental meaning until about the seventeenth century. Aristotle, in fact, referred to his writings as, "first philosophy." For the Greeks, philosophy and science were roughly the same concept because many believed that science was the discovery of first causes—things that did not change (van Inwagen & Sullivan, 2015).

Later, science would branch off into the empirical realm based on new methodologies of discovery and inquiry, and along the way, old terminology shifted and sometimes bowed to new words to describe the complex philosophical systems developing with new ways of thinking (Ihde, 1993; van Inwagen & Sullivan, 2015).

In the broadest sense, *metaphysics* is a branch of philosophy concerned with fundamental nature of reality and ontology is the subfield which explores the abstract concepts of being. The early Greeks equated this search as science probing the fixed aspects of nature meaning concerns about being, firsts, and universal permanence. The Greek word *physis* roughly translates into *nature* in English and captures a sense of permanence and stability, while *techne* refers to production or a sense of making as in art or craft.

Dewey believed that the ancient Greeks and early modern philosophers committed egregious errors in emphasizing *physis* and deemphasizing *techne* because disentangling the two leads to dualisms like mind and body, form and matter, and God and man (Boisvert, 1988). With the gradual collapse of the Greek, and later Roman Empire, Westerners' interest into the nature of the universe ebbed as ecclesiastical concerns arose until roughly the fourteenth century.

Westerners returned to the Aristotelian tradition with the arrival of the Renaissance, but by then the world had become a much more complex, interdependent place with multiple advances in science, humanities, religion, and new ways of thinking. Mirroring the mechanistic advances in science such as inchoate manufacturing and the rise of machines—together with a new modern focus on scientific methodology and inquiry—science became associated with physics, and philosophy with metaphysics. Typical of this philosophical turn was Francis Bacon whose empiricism led to new, modern scientific methodologies and René Descartes who advanced analytical geometry. Both developed philosophies that were concerned with the *conditions* for science. Bacon and Descartes were also among the vanguard ushering in the period of the Enlightenment.

Around the seventeenth century, Renaissance ideals faded as a new era exalting the individual and the power of reason dawned. Jean Jacque Rousseau's *Emile*, David Hume's focus on the psychology of human nature, John Locke's social contract and many other philosophers' works typified this new way of thinking. *Ontology* emerged as a subbranch of metaphysics, meaning firsts, or put another way, resulting in questions related to existence such as: What exists? And, what is it like?

Later, modern *epistemology* surfaced as a theory about what counted as knowledge including the discernment between belief and opinion. By then, philosophers held claim to metaphysics while scientists' discoveries led to great advances in the empirical sciences, which further separated the fields of philosophy and science.

Despite the vast differences among the early Greeks and the Enlightenment philosophers, one common thread permeated all of them as they wrestled with questions related to mind and body, the inner and outer world, God and man, conscious and unconscious, and spectator and object.

As Dewey explained, "The idea that mind and the world of things and persons are two separate spheres and independent realms . . . [is] . . . a theory which philosophically is known as dualism" (*DE*, p. 125). Dewey based his theory on the groundbreaking work of the German philosopher, Georg Wilhelm Friedrich Hegel, who rejected the Cartesian view that self-consciousness is connected to universal truths, and therefore, can transcend any existential physical connections (i.e., mind-body dualism). Instead, Dewey argued that these connections existed in the stable and flux elements of living, which corrected what he saw as the Greek's fascination with the permanent.

Dewey's Theory of Nature

Throughout his lifetime, Dewey rooted many of his arguments in Greek thought, which he especially used as an anchor to elaborate his metaphysics in later years (Anton, 1965). Like the Greeks, Dewey believed that metaphysics as the study of "being" had both universal and specific characteristics depending on the focus; and that the potential to develop specialized knowledge in metaphysics was like other subject matter and could lead to advances in human knowledge and a capacity to make sense of the world.

While the Greeks mainly fixated on the permanent aspects of existence, Dewey emphasized change. Aristotle's metaphysics as "being qua being" is strikingly similar to Dewey's "generic traits of existence" (Hook, 2008, p. 6). The key differences—and one of the reasons Dewey represents a radical departure—is evident in notions of permanence and change, which metaphysicists refer to as "form."

In his later dialogues, Plato began with the premise that humans perceived the world in a faulty and erroneous manner. He conjectured that attractive objects were representations of a permanent and abstract realm of truly beautiful things such as goodness, being, and unity that he called "ideas" or "forms." Therefore, a person can see many beautiful objects, but it is only a representation of the one true beauty independent of time and place (Kraut, 2015).

It is not surprising then that the Greeks equated life with art such as statues and architecture; a person can come to know true beauty, which creates the dualism of the ideal object and spectator. To the Greeks, art was both comfort and refuge from a dangerous and precarious world. Dewey identified Greek form as the basis for their misunderstanding of nature. By focusing on the stable elements, the Greeks and the early modern philosophers like the Realists and Idealists were unable to escape the dualism trap.

Dewey faulted the Realists because they believed the mind mirrored natural entities. He also took issue with the Idealists (although he embraced their arguments in his early years) because they believed reality existed in the mind and that only a universal Reason or God could bridge the abyss between a subject and object. As Dewey's philosophy formed, he infused evolution into his novel naturalism to view humans' continuous interactions with the natural world. In effect, he argued that the interactions constituted reality, and there could be no objective reality beyond human agency.

Dewey's theory of nature contains three principles. First, all beings *experience* the natural world. Second, all beings *interact* with other beings, as well as the environment; and implicitly, beings and the natural environment are changing while interacting. And third, only humans can direct intelligence to consider consequences and *possibility*. Therefore, one constant of being is the relations of change between the organism and the changing environment.

Dewey's metaphysics defines this relationship. He stated, "Qualitative individuality and constant relations, contingency and need, movement and arrest are common traits of all existence" (Dewey, 1929, p. 413). Because some things change faster and slower relative to others, he recognized that stability defines change.

In other words, insofar as all things change, stability can be viewed as a relative moment of apparent stasis in the trajectory of an object. Hence, as we shall see, his metaphysics stakes out a middle position recognizing that things which change slowly are the stable elements while others represent the dynamic aspects of life; and stasis signals a period of inactivity or equilibrium.

THE SOCIAL STUDIES WARS REVISITED

Given the tumultuous history of the social studies, it is not surprising that teachers are often confused about how they should approach the subject matter. Evan's historical account, *The Social Studies Wars: What Should We Teach the Children?* (2004), chronicled the century-old battle to control the curriculum. Acknowledging that many factions have competed for influence over time, the two main opposing camps today are the social studies and social science approach groups (Evans, 2004; Wineburg, 2001).

The question of whether Dewey supported the social studies or a standalone social science curriculum is a proxy war for the larger cultural conflicts around what the curriculum should be and who should control it. Key differences between the social studies and social science groups include what courses should be offered in schools, the purpose and source of the curriculum materials, and the arrangement of the subject matter as either disciplinary or interdisciplinary.

Whereas the social studies formal curriculum is focused on social issues and comprised of social science subjects such as history, geography, government, economics, psychology, sociology, and others in a traditional sense, it also can incorporate courses like peer mediation, current events, or pre-law, among infinite possibilities. Another key difference is the social science approach is more concerned with the integrity of the various disciplines, as well as the sources of material. The social studies, conversely, emphasizes student interests and engaging in interdisciplinary inquiry across the humanities.

The split between the two approaches also manifests itself in the arrangement of the curriculum in the early grades. The social studies follows an expanding horizon beginning with the young student's study of family structures and emanating out into the wider community and world. The social science advocates, on the other hand, propose stand-alone social science and history courses where myths and storytelling help captivate young learners (Egan, 1980, 1983; Thornton, 2005).

The perceived paradox of Dewey's ambivalence about the social studies curriculum considering his interdisciplinary approach to curriculum presents a golden opportunity to put Deweyan philosophy into action. Did he support a traditional, social science approach to history and geography because he addressed them distinctly in *Democracy and Education* (1916)?

Answering this question is vitally important because if the social studies teacher educators—the formal researchers and scholars in the discipline—cannot settle on a definitive answer, the field will never achieve its full philosophical and intellectual bearings and will be forever fragmented. The consequence of this divide has been a confused and incompetent curriculum, which has led to tepid student interest and mediocre learning.

Dewey's Philosophy in Action

Dewey freed philosophy from the intellectual class and pushed it out into the world, where anyone could roll up her or his sleeves and get to the work of solving real problems. Deweyan philosophy, in its fullest meaning, is a methodical and rigorous means to examine, critique, rethink, and act upon a perceived problem. It is never the answer, but serves as the conduit for examining more options, deliberating consequences against a larger context, in an extended period or in relation to some underlying forces. Dewey believed that philosophy should serve all individuals and society. Thus, schools became a major focus of his endeavors.

The centerpiece of Dewey's theory of nature is the live creature's experience with the natural world. Ontologically, anything that exists is a potential resource for *an event*, every individual *interacts* in some way with other things that exist, and all natural existences are *histories*. A human being continuous with nature is constantly adjusting and adapting to the vicissitudes of life and striving for peace, harmony, and stability.

A central characteristic of existence is change and stability, and "what something 'really is' is a function of the changes, alterations, and reactions to surroundings that it undergoes" (Boisvert, 1988, p. 133). The central purpose of schools, according to Dewey, was to socialize young people to adapt in this social milieu, which in educational terms means that students should utilize the full breadth of all subject matter to study current social conditions with an eye for improving the future. In this way, the curriculum becomes a content *and* method for enlarging individual experience for thriving in the world.

Dewey turned everything upside down by reframing the philosophical questions in an evolutionary way. For him, *the object* is a specific ontological term for something that results from an inquiry within *an* experience. Unlike Plato who believed that ideal beauty could be known, Dewey hypothesized that an individual can have *an* experience with aesthetic qualities as a production process rather than *come to know* that ideal beauty beyond human cognition.

In this system of ideas, whether Dewey supported a social studies curriculum or favored a social science approach to instruction does not result in a paradox because the question is not logical in the context of Deweyan thought, particularly considering the formal curricula and the needs of young learners. Dewey (*CC*) explained,

> From the study of the child, it is a question of seeing how his experience already contains within itself elements—facts and truths—of just the same sort as those entering into the formulated study; and, what is of more importance, of how it contains within itself the attitudes, the motives, and the interests which have operated in developing and organizing the subject-matter to the plane which it now occupies. From the side of the studies, it is a question of interpreting them as outgrowths of forces operating in the child's life, and of discovering the steps that intervene between the child's present experience and their richer maturity. (p. 109)

In other words, the teacher must interpret the formal studies—the disciplinary organizations of curriculum—in a way that recognizes the inherent connections to the needs and capacities of the child.

The Instrumental Nature of Social Studies and the Social Sciences

Social studies and history or geography are not mutually exclusive enterprises. In fact, Dewey conceived all disciplinary concepts as instruments for sustained action on the world. Rather than an either/or question resulting in a paradox being continuous with nature invites the question, "How do the disciplines interpenetrate each other?" In Deweyan terms, you cannot have *a social study* without tapping into our forebears' experiences about human associations (i.e., history) and their interactions with the natural environment (i.e., geography).

In educational equivalents, you cannot have a social studies subject matter without a formal curriculum of facts and concepts in history and geography. However, teachers must select and manipulate history, geography, and all social science disciplines in a way that expands an individual's capacity "to perceive the spatial, the natural, connections of an ordinary act" and "to gain in power to recognize human connections" (*DE*, p. 157).

In fact, Dewey (*PP*) later expressed great faith in the potential for the newly emergent social sciences to operate as "an apparatus for conducting investigation, and for recording and interpreting (organizing) its results" (p. 203). He optimistically forecasted that individuals would use the tools of these disciplinary constructs to form their beliefs using evidence rather than custom and caprice.

Dewey suggested this happens most effectively when a skilled teacher develops aims, cultivates student interest, and particularly for young children, engages them in active occupations. Consequently, concluding that Dewey supported a social science approach in schools reveals a fundamental lack of understanding in his theory of knowledge and the proper role of the formal curriculum in the ongoing work of human advancement.

Misunderstanding the Middle Position

Dewey's theory of nature offers a middle position between respecting the traditional subject curriculum and acknowledging the vital role the teacher plays in enlarging students' experiences, which will have implications later when this work addresses the Common Core Standards (CCS). For now though, the point is that educators misunderstand him because he created a novel ontology that contextualized disciplinary knowledge in human history and took the position that thinking is always rooted in contemporary problems which are framed by the current intellectual standards in form and content.

In Deweyan thought, history and geography "are the information studies par excellence of the schools" (*DE*, p. 158). Yet, as we have seen, it would be a critical mistake to conclude that Dewey merely endorsed the subject matter as things to be learned. In ontological terms, thinking of the curriculum content as something students internalize creates a misleading philosophical dualism that emphasizes the stable or permanent elements of the curriculum and denigrates the active construction of meaningful knowledge.

In fact, Dewey barely concealed his derision when he commented, "The words 'history' and 'geography' suggest simply the matter which has been traditionally sanctioned in the schools" (p. 158). Formal traditional school curriculum is a static, disconnected collection of information that *only offers the potential to build a student's civic capacity with the guidance of the skilled teacher*, something that will be explored in more depth throughout the next chapter.

Humans generate knowledge within social activities, and what they deem culturally important, they pass from one generation to the next. Dewey advanced a middle position where the growth process reconciles the adult aims, values, and meanings in the formal curriculum with the immature experiences and interests of the child.

DEVELOPING A DEMOCRATIC VISION FOR TEACHING SOCIAL STUDIES

In the context of Dewey's vast writings, *Democracy and Education* (1916) represents his finest polemic against the traditional approach in education of rote memorization, recitation, and subject matter disconnected from students' lives. It is also his most complete philosophical exposition of instrumentalism and education where he painstakingly laid bare the connections among life, education, growth, and society.

Later, in response to reader confusion and a reaction to those who interpreted his ideas as advocating student interests to run rampant, he composed *Experience and Education* (1938), a spare and concise version of his main arguments. Nonetheless, *Democracy and Education* (1916) has persisted as one of the greatest philosophical and practical treatises about curriculum ever written. In the opening pages, Dewey presented his case that the purpose of schools is to prepare young people for community life and to act with intelligence in the world.

Dewey recognized that most education, or an individual's growth, occurs historically and practically outside of formal school structures, but in modern times, only schools offer the universal means to educate young people. This progressive perspective emphasizes a broad definition of democracy that includes both the political and social aspects of acting in the world and he was particularly concerned with creating active citizens.

Dewey presciently explicated a radical, reformist impulse in his reasoning: first, the modern world is too complex for families and clans to take on this role; second, schools potentially provide a counterbalance and corrective measure to the harmful experiences a young person encounters in daily living. And most surprisingly given the times, schools are the great equalizer for the poor, people of color, and those from minority religious and ethnic backgrounds.

This period represents Dewey's pivot to an emphasis on radical, liberal democracy. Before 1916, he alleged that hierarchically organized, mediating, environmental factors determined whether a person more or less turned out savage or civilized. After, he argued that plurality enriched the conditions for all learners, and by extension, enhanced citizenship and democracy (Fallace, 2011).

Dewey asserted, "The intermingling in the school of youth of different races, differing religions, and unlike customs creates for all a new and broader environment" (*DE*, p. 21). He staked out a forward-looking position that resonates with contemporary views and efforts in stark contrast to the prevailing social attitudes of the time.

The Central Problem of the Social Studies

In social studies education programs today, professors typically ask preservice teachers to (1) reflect and develop a philosophy of education, or a set of interrelated beliefs about why and how to teach social studies to children and (2) a rationale for what they are teaching. Further complicating the picture, a philosophy statement also embodies interests and dispositions. Despite concerted efforts on the part of professors and professional organizations like National Council for the Social Studies (NCSS), much of the teaching and learning in social studies classrooms does not mirror a democratic, reconstructionist Deweyan vision.

This and other critical issues have plagued the field since its inception. As Misco (2014) observed, "[S]ocial studies education often suffers from a perversion of mission, existing as declarative, atomized, disconnected, and irrelevant content, with standardized measures of knowledge and value-added assessment movements further undermining any resemblance of social studies" (p. 241). Whether one points to high-stakes tests, the challenges of classroom management or any other contributing factor, the reality remains that it is easier for social studies teachers to regress to or remain mired in a traditional mode of curriculum and instruction.

Misco and Shiveley (2010) define dispositions as what results when "interests become habitual and crystallized" (p. 122). They also turn to Dewey to create a taxonomy based on open-mindedness, wholeheartedness, and responsibility to combat the marginalization of the social studies and the all-consuming focus on standards and assessment, as well as the unwieldy breadth of the curriculum. A first step to establish coherence in the social studies curriculum may be for prospective and in-service teachers to devise a personal rationale statement.

Developing a Rationale for Teaching Social Studies

A recommended first step in developing a vision for social studies teaching would be for every candidate to construct a rationale. The idea of social studies teachers developing a rationale or purpose has been around at least since the 1970s (Newmann, 1977; Newmann & Oliver, 1970; Shaver, 1977;

Shaver & Strong, 1982) to address disparate beliefs about educating for democratic citizenship, as well as the daily constraints of teaching (Barton & Levstik, 2004; Dinkelman, 2009; Engle & Ochoa-Becker, 1988; Ochoa-Becker, 1996).

To engage in a consensus view among social studies theorists requires significant disciplinary knowledge, as well as knowledge of current and persistent social issues. Consistent with Dewey's focus on problem solving, developing a rationale is conceptual and interdisciplinary, rather than chronological, disciplinary, and topical. A recommendation for a high-quality rationale would look for:

- Key democratic values (such as freedom, equality, due process, justice, etc.).
- The nature of knowledge (interdisciplinary focus on issues with supporting content from the social science disciplines and the humanities).
- The nature of teachers and teaching (focusing on the shift from authoritarian to facilitative, probing, and interactive teaching).
- The nature of learners and learning (intellectual development and cultural background of students).
- The nature of society, domestic and global, including all aspects of diversity. (Ochoa-Becker, 1996, p. 7)

The focus is on student-centered learning, goal setting, and engaging with contemporary social problems.

Social studies scholars have proposed various curriculum models throughout the past several decades, and they have several Deweyan characteristics in common related to the nature of knowledge, teachers and teaching, learners and learning, and society. First, they all begin with the premise that knowledge is tentative and subject to further interrogation. Second, the teacher's role is critical for facilitating an interactive experience whether through student-led initiatives or other formats such as teacher-led Socratic discourse. Third, learning is an active, holistic process involving a person's entire being where mental activity is inseparable from physical bodily activity. And fourth, they rest on the assumption that a democracy can only survive if the citizens solve problems and resolve conflicts (Ochoa-Becker, 1996).

Recent research suggests that beginning teachers can benefit from crafting purpose statements (Hawley, 2010; Hawley & Crowe, 2016; Hawley, Pifel, & Jordan, 2012). When teachers closely hew to them, they can provide structure, link purpose with practice, and result in an enhanced state of professionalism. The need for a purposive rationale cannot be overstated as Hawley and Crowe (2016) explain,

> While integrating rationale development, a program's purposes must be considered. Is it enough for preservice teachers to demonstrate the ability to plan for

and enact engaging lessons? Is it enough for them to demonstrate a strong command of social studies content? Is it enough for them to demonstrate professionalism? We propose it is not. If preservice teachers do not, or cannot, demonstrate a commitment to teaching social studies or they cannot or are not interested in teaching social studies for the common good (Barton & Levstik, 2004), perhaps they should not be social studies teachers. (p. 441)

It is likely that veteran teachers would also benefit from reflective rationale construction because whether they realize it or not, they teach from their values.

A starting point for any social studies rationale begins with values related to democracy. Democracy is messy and difficult to maintain. It requires extraordinary fortitude to build communities where citizens cooperate, deliberate, compromise, and through consensus, solve the problems of daily living. The democratic system is built on a strong faith in reason, which is precisely what Dewey explicated nearly a century ago when he identified the problem of the public (*PP*).

Dewey's radical democratic philosophy offers a road map for constructing a vision of effective social studies teaching and learning, based on an organic, dynamic rationale that should constantly evolve to meet emerging demands (see table 1.1). As part of the process, teachers should be able to provide tentative answers to the guiding questions, many of which will gain added relevance as they are grounded throughout this book. The central feature of democratic classrooms is the opportunity for students to study social problems.

Creating the conditions for students to study social problems today and throughout history is not politically partisan. In fact, as Dewey admonished us many years ago, it should not become an opportunity to indoctrinate students (Dewey, 1946). However, it should present an opportunity for students to develop their individual political identities together with the full range of possibilities for active citizenship.

To that end, a social studies classroom should resemble a community where teachers gain a deep understanding of their students' interests, needs, and capacities. The teachers then use this information to design inquiry learning activities recognizing that this method of study and conjoint communication is firmly anchored in our human evolutionary history. Learning means that students encounter new situations that are problematic and require novel solutions. Habit no longer suffices and old beliefs must be altered or discarded if one is to grow. Moreover, as individuals tussle with problems and reflect on possible solutions, they are considering how those solutions affect others.

Teachers should always consider their vision as a work in progress and a Herculean feat to implement and maintain. However, the disciplinary-based

Table 1.1. Using Deweyan Philosophy to Construct a Social Studies Teacher Rationale

Traits of Deweyan Philosophy	Connections to the Social Studies Curriculum	Questions to Guide Rationale Building
1. Accessibility	The foundation of the social studies curriculum is built upon a Deweyan rationale of interdisciplinary problem solving. Every individual has the potential to use instrumental philosophy to shape problems, select tools, and evaluate consequences.	• In what ways can you design and justify a curriculum to include multiple opportunities and ways for students to identify, study, and offer solutions to social problems? • How can you facilitate the inclusion of diverse resources and perspectives?
2. Being continuous with natural world	The content of the social studies curriculum changes over time reflecting the current, valued knowledge and skills. Further, the teacher provides opportunities for the students to draw on all the social sciences, humanities, and other subject areas as the students engage with social issues requiring them to "use" history, and then conjecture into the future as they evaluate competing claims, render judgments, and negotiate meaning.	• How can you adapt your rationale to changing conditions? • In what ways can you promote academic risk-taking and idea experimentation? • How will you organize students for maximum democratic discourse and deliberation? • What will your classroom look and sound like?
3. Experience as the minimum unit of analysis	Most experiences with the world are non cognitive and habitual. Indeterminate situations force students to cognitively transcend habit and engage in problem solving where content and methods are unified in experience.	• How can your selection of content and methods facilitate problem solving? • How will you promote more critical thinking and reflective inquiry? • How will you evaluate students?
4. Democracy as an ethical/moral ideal	The social studies citizenship mission is to prepare students for associated living where they have opportunities to study current problems and consider solutions and their consequences as they affect others.	• In what ways will you guide students to identify social problems? • To what extent will you place controls in your classroom to avoid indoctrinating students to one point of view?
5. Purpose/reform of schools	Students will be able to discover their interests and teachers will design problem-based learning experiences based on those interests.	• How can you make students aware of their interests? • How will you create differentiated learning experiences based on student interests, needs, and capacities?

alternative of teaching history and social science courses like we find at the college level perpetuates a system that has disenfranchised generations of young people and threatens the core of democracy in the long term as we descend into "idiocy" and personal interest usurps the needs of community (Parker, 2003).

SUMMARY

This chapter debunks the myth that Dewey presented a paradox in his approach to problem solving and his alleged support for traditional history and social science curricula. In effect, the paradox is a symptom of social studies educators misunderstanding the philosophical foundations of Deweyan thought. Clarifying Dewey's philosophy and its connections to the social studies provides the *why* and *how* of the interaction among students, teachers and the learning environment, something sorely lacking in a bifurcated field with factions competing for control of the curriculum.

In addition to the sharp differences between the social studies and social science advocates, there are cleavages related to many other issues including whether social studies classes should be stand-alone or linked with other social science or humanity courses; the gap between theory and practice; what counts as history; whether students should be using technology to learn social studies and how; and many others (Evans, 2004, 2010; Lybarger, 1983; Wronski, 1993). These are not just societal problems; they are also philosophical challenges. Reframing the issues in Deweyan philosophy can also point the way for solutions and bring to the surface a variety of theories.

The central problem of the social studies, though, is not the same as societal problems. Rather, it is the fact that in most social studies classrooms, teachers still follow a traditional, disciplinary approach to teaching the curriculum resulting in student disinterest and lost opportunities for instruction in active citizenship. Without a clear philosophical foundation, the field suffers. A vision for social studies teachers begins with a rationale firmly rooted in Dewey's democracy.

The social studies curriculum is a young curriculum, and given its genesis in Dewey's system of ideas, it makes sense to turn to his theories for guidance and curriculum making. Theories are composed of concepts and principles, which are used to explain phenomena and predict future consequences. They also serve as the foundation for scientific investigation. To that end, each chapter of this book is structured with an emphasis on a major, interrelated, Deweyan theory: (1) Nature; (2) Curriculum; (3) Experience; (4) Interest and Morals; (5) Inquiry; and (6) Citizenship.

Chapter 2

Curriculum

Focus Questions:

1 Where does school curriculum come from?
2 Why do teacher beliefs matter?
3 What are the elements of curriculum structures that support a vision for learning?

The ordinary experiences of our ancestors supply the formal school curriculum. While many people think of curriculum content as merely information and skills to learn in various areas such as English, mathematics, and literature, Dewey (*CC*) viewed subject matter as intellectualized, powerful, and valuable organizations of knowledge impregnated with methods and grounded in our forebears' experiences,

> On the face of it, the various studies, arithmetic, geography, language, botany, etc., are themselves experience—they are that of the race. They embody the cumulative outcome of the efforts, the strivings, and the successes of the human race generation after generation. They present this, not as a mere accumulation, not as a miscellaneous heap of separate bits of experience, but in some organized and systematized way—that is, as reflectively formulated. (p. 109)

Further, Dewey explicated that the role of the teacher is to "psychologize" (*CC*, p. 117) these formal organizations of information.

Psychologizing the curriculum, Dewey explained, is "keep[ing] in mind the double aspect of subject matter," (*CC*, pp. 117–18) which in one view is an adult organization of information, and in the other, a potential object for the young learner to *use* in experience only if the teacher modifies and adopts it in a way to match the needs and capacity of the student.

Expressed another way, teachers "reinterpret the fundamental concepts and methods of the respective disciplines in accessible, engaging, and powerful ways for students" (Smith III & Girod, 2003, p. 295). This can only happen if teachers begin with critical reflection.

Effective teachers evaluate their own belief systems, confirm current school conditions with an eye for creating communities of learners, and discover their students' wants, interests, and capacities in their efforts to create active and authentic learning experiences. And because our ancestors' experiences as embodied in disciplinary knowledge (e.g., history, geography, mathematics, physics, etc.) represent their doings and makings in response to the human condition, psychologizing the curriculum also means that young children should learn at least some of the ways our ancestors have met human challenges, some of which are ongoing through active occupations.

More than in any other school subject area, the social studies curriculum inherently embodies Deweyan thought (Saxe, 1992). Over eight decades, builders of formal social studies curriculum intelligently organized the content, offering learners *the potential* to study current problems using an inquiry approach to learning and decision making. The emphasis on students' interactions with the research and decision-making aspect also reflects the domain's aim for creating effective citizens.

However, because the curriculum consists of infinitely boundless content areas of history, the social sciences, and other humanities, the teacher's interaction with the disciplinary organizations is essential for the selection of *what* students will learn, as well as *how* they should learn it. Unfortunately, school conditions have never been truly hospitable for implementing a Deweyan approach to learning social studies in a widespread way, and teachers' beliefs about the purpose the social studies may influence whether they implement an active, Deweyan approach (Goodlad, 1984; Tyack, 1974).

In Dewey's curriculum theory, the teacher plays a central role in facilitating student learning. This chapter explores the evolutionary sources of school subject matter, and consequently, how content and methods become unified in experience. Next, a discussion ensues about why teacher beliefs matter, and how they relate to social studies aims.

Next, the discussion pivots to the three pedagogical traditions in the social studies—Citizen Transmission, Social Scientist, and Reflective Inquiry type teachers—and concludes that the Citizenship Transmission teachers have dominated since the beginning, and probably consolidated more power following the 1990s history teaching wars.

And finally, while acknowledging the political and structural realities of schools, the chapter ends with suggestions offering social studies teachers specific structures to support a Deweyan curriculum followed by an illustration of how it has the potential to expand a learner's experience. *A vision for social studies teachers is to analyze their beliefs about the purpose and aim of the social studies, and then experiment with non-chronological curriculum structures so students have myriad opportunities for conceptual learning.*

THE SOURCES OF SCHOOL SUBJECT MATTER

The ultimate source of curriculum is human social activity, which science traces back to pre-humans who developed diets based on meat and cooking. Instead of spending nearly all their waking hours foraging for plant food, early hominids consumed enough calories to live in extended social arrangements. Moreover, the calorically dense foods allowed their brains to grow larger and more complex with increased neurons; and consequently, the interaction of increased cognitive activity and associated living produced the conditions for an extraordinary human evolution (Carmody, Weintraub, & Wrangham, 2011; Fonseca-Azevedo & Herculano-Houzel, 2012).

Modern humans arrived relatively recently—perhaps in the last 50,000 to 200,000 years—and with them they carried all the vestiges of prior associations. Despite the vast cultural differences that developed across humanity, being human also signified many commonalities forged in natural selection from requiring the basic needs for survival of food, shelter, and air to how humans faced challenges in securing these necessities (Diamond, 1997). In the process, individuals uniquely accumulated the habits of thinking and further adaptation in the social sphere.

At the same time, language and other means of communication developed as a way for humans to make sense of the world. For Dewey, all logical explanations are rooted in evolution and the story of humankind is of the social interaction with the natural environment. Put another way, life is a process of continuous, cumulative experiences, and some are so valuable, our ancestors identified and passed them down to successive generations.

Before the invention of writing, group elders orally and demonstrably passed down culturally valuable experiences to the younger members. Historically, much of this transmission concerned basic survival such as what types of plants were edible and which ones were poisonous or how to build a boat using locally available materials. As conditions changed, some experiences lost relevance as new ones emerged.

Other people's experiences socialize young people to get on in the world; experience is not mere information, but rather what people *did* and what they *underwent* for survival and growth. In Dewey's interpretation of history, individuals take these valuable experiences that have been handed down and adapt them to changing conditions.

Human Participation in Nature's Rhythms

In the beginning, the evolutionary journey commenced with human participation in nature's rhythms, where primitive human experience also laid the foundation for the arts. Not surprisingly then, one finds Dewey's most cogent narrative about human evolution in *Art as Experience* (1934). Before all modern conveniences, humans adjusted and adapted in harmony with the natural world.

The rising and setting of the sun, the ebb and flow of the seas, the arrival of the quenching summer rains, the phases of the moon, the reproductive cycle of animals, and all the other pulses of life provided the backdrop, foil, and accomplice in the stories of people's lives. Within the longer natural rhythms, our forebears developed agriculture and animal husbandry, which also included a system for measuring time based on astronomy providing guidance when to plant, till, and harvest, as well as when to shorn, breed, and birth the animals.

Ever-curious and forever encountering challenges and obstacles, over a vast period of time, people experimented, innovated, and measured smaller units within the longer rhythms while engaging in the "patting, chipping, molding, cutting, pounding" of the crafts (*AE*, p. 154). With the working of clay, metals, wood, leather, and fibers, they constructed the utensils for solving problems and fashioned objects to satisfy their ritualistic needs.

These activities later became formalized as occupations such as baker, blacksmith, cooper, and cobbler, but perhaps more importantly, they served as a means to survive, thrive, and make collective sense of the world. Social occupations allowed humans to adapt and grow in a changing world. Further, they shaped the social order and provided the cultural conditions for communities of knowledge builders. Today, active occupations are particularly valuable as manual activities for younger children to learn ways of knowing.

When individuals impose their unique rhythms on changes where they do not normally exist, or when people unite elements of the crafts with a human voice and controlled body movements, they create spatial and temporal fine art. Spatial creations, such as temples and sculptures, possess rhythmic symmetry while temporal ones, such as music and dance, employ rhythm in the plainest sense. Literature emerges an exemplar of the fine arts because it originated from commercial letters and developed into an intense form of communication based on others' experiences. Moreover, these arts provided the conditions for modern science.

In the ancient Greek world, science and art were equivalent concepts because knowledge was a fixed, immediate entity that one's mind could contemplate and possess. At some point around the time when the Renaissance yielded to the Scientific Revolution, art and science parted ways when the scientific community embraced an experimental approach to constructing knowledge, which meant that knowledge could never attain a final, idealized form.

Historically, the physical sciences developed from the craft arts and the mental sciences evolved from the political arts. The former provided the formulae for the natural rhythms of life such as Newton's theory of gravitation and Kepler's laws of planetary motion. At about the same time, Kant, Locke, and many other Enlightenment thinkers advanced elements of psychology, although Dewey often pointed to assertions he found erroneous and used them to frame his own ideas about relational aspects of experience (e.g., *DE*, *PP*, and *LTI*).

The schism between art and science—or more accurately, the consequence of the arts having birthed the sciences—resulted in an explosion of knowledge and the rise of the scientific method, which reduced all natural existences to means. It also led to an exponential growth of knowledge as humans measured increasingly smaller rhythms such as molecules, atoms, particles and subatomic particles, and waves. Likewise, how scientists and philosophers made sense of the world also shifted from immediate, primary experience to reflection and abstraction. They devised symbols and formulae to explain these newly discovered rhythms.

When individuals engage in reflective activities using patterns and formulae in the sciences, they transcend perceptions in existence, and science became a means and method for "making sure" (*EN*, p. 154). Scientific discovery also yields laws, and within the most generalized universal statements, results can be formulated in the abstract terms of pure mathematics, as abstract quantities, divorced from any reference to the sensuous particulars being counted. For example, 100 loaves of bread for 50 people is a statement of existence suggesting one-half loaf of bread per individual. However, 100 divided by 50 is pure mathematics, not connected to any real existence.

Ultimately, any knowledge passed down from generation to generation originated in our ancestors' interactions with nature. Further, the selection, arrangement, and transmission of the experiences meant that those who came before us applied intelligence to the arrangement and organization of those valued experiences, and unwittingly supplied a solution to the philosophical problem of dualisms.

The Unity of Teaching and Learning

Dewey's metaphysics conceptualizes individuals as continuous with nature. Within this network of ideas, Dewey and other pragmatists solved the dualism conundrum, which forced philosophers to argue things like the mind operated in a separate realm from the body. Stated another way, dualisms forced philosophers to argue for some sort of divine intervention or higher power like Reason in overcoming these divides in existence.

Dewey argued that subject matter in the sense of formal school curriculum ought to be a logical, organized arrangement of information, concepts, facts, principles, and all other valued experiences from the past that our ancestors already psychologized using intelligence. In effect, he argued that the selection and arrangement of curriculum is imbued with methods.

If they are not, he asserted, then one either believes someone or something stamps the facts and concepts on the mind or the mind seizes them; that is, one believes they are not human constructs or creations of human interaction with the social and natural world. With traditional philosophy, he continued to explain, one conceptualizes the mind as autonomous from the physical body. A further implication, he surmised, is that learning is independent of disciplinary knowledge as a tool for acting on the world and people can master a *general* methodology.

Clearly, a historian operates differently from an organic chemist, and following Dewey's logic, that is because the disciplinary knowledge of the historian—artifacts, documents, testimony—is intellectualized in the subject matter differently from the rules and complex equations of hydrogen and carbon-based reactions of the chemist's domain. Moreover, in this sense disciplinary knowledge is an external object—a tool—one can *use* in experience, as we expect students to do analogously with the formal curriculum.

Dewey qualitatively described how a human being *uses* subject matter. He described "thinking" as "a directed movement of subject matter to a completing issue" (*DE*, p. 125). The thinking occurs within the context of a perceived problem and in the process of some type of inquiry, and then *subject matter* takes on a different (but not separate) meaning within an experience.

As the subject matter is *in use*, it is a most efficient method for thinking because it is intellectualized in selection and arrangement. Further, when subject matter is being used method can never be external to the materials, which is the *context* of the methods or content.

As an example, Dewey described the method of a pianist with the end goal of performing a composition, and then stated, "Order is found in the disposition of acts which use the piano and hands and brain so as to achieve the result intended" (*DE*, p. 126). The pianist example is akin to a historian tasked with reconstructing an understanding of a historical event from the Civil War.

For the historian, the pen and paper, or computer and software, act as instruments as she methodically examines photographs, letters, public archives, and secondary sources and composes a narrative—contextualizing, comparing, critically evaluating the attributions, and all the other elements she uses to construct a viable interpretation. She does not write extraneous musings.

She concomitantly utilizes the materials at hand, shuffles items around, types something, consults another document, and so on. She does not compose solely with her mind, but with her hands, brain, and myriad associated acts. The acts are part of *an* experience with an end-in-view.

To Dewey, generalizing means returning to metaphysics and placing a situation in evolutionary change. As he enthused, "Experience is the perception of the connection between something tried and something undergone in consequence is a process" (*DE*, p. 126). In less obtuse language, the process involves how a person acts, how the environment changes about her because of the acts, and finally, how her understanding changes because of the acts and their consequences.

One cannot separate the physical and psychical acts in experience. The historian who creates a well-regarded book about the Civil War does not offer distinct credit to computer software or primary sources. Rather, the philosophical frame of reference is *a situation* where the historian's purposeful methodology and subject matter unify in the *process* of *interpreting, creating*, and *transmitting* while working toward an envisioned end. The phases of experience involve the interplay of the mental and physical aspects of existence, which negates the dualism trap. Furthermore, the situation highlights the oversimplification of the phrase, "learning by doing."

When a person reflects within an experience, she intrinsically forms a distinction between her attitudes and the objects to which she directs the attitudes. Dewey illustrated this point with an example of eating. When a person eats, she does not separate food from chewing, tasting, and swallowing. However, if she reflects (e.g., inquires whether the food is healthy given her circumstances) upon the act, she may consider the nutritional value, the caloric content, or whether she is allergic to certain ingredients (*DE*).

Dewey classified this distinction as the "what" (e.g., the properties of the food) with the "how" (e.g., the eater's perception of allergic reaction and eating), which is the same distinction between subject matter and methods. When a person has *an* experience, meaning "a single continuous interaction of a great diversity (literally countless in number) of energies" (*DE*, p. 127), and reflects upon it, she divines a distinction in thinking, which however, is not a distinction in existence. *Dualisms originate because philosophers fail to recognize the discrimination between reflection and existence as part of an integrated experience.*

THE SOCIAL STUDIES TEACHER'S INTERACTION

Staking a middle position, Dewey respected the formal canons as codifications of human knowledge while acknowledging the yawning gulf between the adult, organized bodies of subject matter (e.g., disciplinary knowledge) and the experiences of young people. The teacher's charge is to bridge this chasm. Dewey believed that it was not sufficient to concentrate on children's interests in isolation, but rather he viewed the formal curriculum as something that provides direction for disciplining those interests.

Since its inception over seventy-five years ago, we have never truly implemented a widespread social studies approach. In fact, the approach is "moribund" and more like the social science curriculum of the nineteenth century "existing as declarative, atomized, disconnected, and irrelevant content" (Misco, 2014, p. 241). Over the years, scholars documented many reasons why teachers have resisted a social studies stance to learning.

Some cite culture and the contradictory demands placed on social studies teachers (Evans, 2004; Goodlad, 1984). Because of federal testing mandates in math and literacy, the narrowing curriculum leaves precious time for social studies instruction especially for younger learners; and by middle school, most social studies classes are stand-alone history, government, and economics together with a smattering of social science courses like sociology and psychology (Thornton, 2005).

Students often rank the social studies as one of their least favorite subject matters (Goodlad, 1984; Schug, 1982). Bland textbooks and high-stakes tests become the proxy curriculum. In the New York City school district, marginal learners—who were often high-needs, high-poverty, and ethnically diverse—experienced some of the most mind-numbing social studies instruction imaginable.

Many of these students enroll multiple times in a social studies class aptly named, "Regents Review Course," in the hopes of passing the two social studies Regents exams in Global History and Geography, as well as U.S. History and Government. The students laboriously drill with multiple-choice items and Document-based question (DBQ) essays similar to those found on the exams following a textbook compiled to mimic the test items, which unfortunately is all too common (Misco, 2010). Passing these high-stakes tests allow students to graduate with a Regents diploma opening avenues for further educational opportunities.

Social studies teacher educators have commiserated for some time over the paucity of powerful social studies instruction and the disparity between what preservice teachers experience in a teacher preparation program and what they do in the field. Some suggest that professional development directed at preservice teachers can enhance the curriculum (Adler, 1991, 1994; Hursh, 1994; Ross, 1994; Ross & Hannay, 1986).

Teacher Beliefs and Enacting a Social Studies Curriculum

At least three potential reasons exist today as to why most elementary and social studies teachers do not enact a Deweyan curriculum as advocated by

The NCSS where students encounter "pervasive and enduring social issues" connected to their lives, "conduct inquiry, develop and display data, synthesize findings, and make judgments" while "apply[ing] value-based reasoning when addressing problems" and "develop[ing] fair-mindedness" (National Council for the Social Studies, 2016, p. 181).

Teachers either possess a rigid belief system in which they are unwilling to entertain a Deweyan scheme; they do not know how to implement the curriculum; or they do know how and may be willing to attempt it, but the school environment is aversive or unsupportive for enactment. Dewey aimed his philosophy squarely at education because so much of what had been done in the past was based solely on custom and tradition, and reflected in the attitudes of officials and decision makers.

To engage in reflective inquiry, an individual must be open to perceiving the problem and challenging her own assumptions and beliefs. Dewey extensively presented critical reflection in *How We Think* (1910) where he described all thinking as beginning with a problem or "a state of perplexity, hesitation, doubt" (p. 9) followed by an inquiry to either support or debunk the *belief*, which Pring (2007) defined as, "The settled state of mind about how to act, and about what to expect as a consequence of acting" (p. 68). Perhaps many preservice and in-service teachers do not become reflective inquiry practitioners because of their entrenched belief systems.

The Intersection of Beliefs and Teacher Preparation

The research on teacher beliefs embodies three overarching perspectives. First, some researchers postulate that beliefs are established early in life, and when someone enters a teacher preparation program, those beliefs remain robust and predict future behaviors (Lortie, 1975; Richardson, 2003). A second perspective suggests that a teacher education program has a profound effect on shaping teacher actions as belief systems accommodate new experiences (Bondy et al., 2007; Elby & Hammer, 2010; Hart, 2002).

And third, others conclude that while some elements of an education program do influence teacher performance, the influence is modest at best (Adler, 1991; Darling-Hammond, 2000; Dinkelman, 1999). Underlying these three perspectives are questions about what distinguishes beliefs from knowledge, the composition of attitudes, belief interactions and beliefs related to preservice and novice teachers.

When beliefs are arranged in a permanent way around some entity or condition inciting an individual to act in a predisposed way, they form an attitude. Each of the underlying attitudinal beliefs contains three parts: the cognitive, affective, and behavioral components. The cognitive component represents an individual's degree of certainty related to the belief such as one being 90 percent sure that a mountain range traverses Italy or that smoking cigarettes is always bad.

The affective component allows the individual to express an intensity of feeling about the object of the belief, or juxtapose it with other objects of the belief. An example would be a student addressing the validity of a proposition such as, "All wars are bad." The student may then present a nuanced argument related to some wars being justified with positive outcomes, while at the same time, others being harmful and executed with devious intentions and resulting in disastrous consequences.

The third component, behavioral, means that the individual *potentially* acts under certain conditions. One may believe that the minimum wage should be raised, and yet not act on promoting the position until a family member experiences hardship. In sum, a subset of interacting beliefs can form an attitude (Rokeach, 1968).

In addition to the formation of attitudes, beliefs can also interact with other beliefs in myriad ways. Teachers may hold beliefs about practice, pedagogy, the students, and the school among others. Therefore, Pajares (1992) suggested a context-based approach to examining beliefs such as:

> beliefs about confidence to affect students' performances (teacher efficacy), about the nature of knowledge (epistemological beliefs), about causes of teachers' or students' performance (attributions, locus of control, motivation, writing apprehension, math anxiety), about perceptions of self and feeling of self-worth (self-concept, self-esteem), about confidence to perform specific tasks (self-efficacy). There are also educational beliefs about specific subjects or disciplines (reading instruction, the nature of reading, whole language). (p. 316)

The social studies literature is infused with evidence that teachers' contextual beliefs profoundly influence their curriculum approaches.

Social studies teachers' beliefs affect what they teach and how including their roles as curriculum gatekeepers (Thornton, 2005), their perceptions of high-stakes tests (Grant, 2003; Saye, 2013), beliefs about technology integration (Bai & Ertmer, 2008; Sadaf, Newby, & Ertmer, 2012; VanFossen & Waterson, 2008), and even their beliefs about how best to integrate the knowledge, values, and skills to promote effective citizenship as either Citizenship Transmitters, Social Scientists, or Reflective Inquirers (Barr et al., 1978).

Aims Talk Revisited

In *Teaching Social Studies That Matters: Curriculum for Active Learning*, Thornton (2005) describes a teacher's choices from a Deweyan perspective. In chapter 1, he introduces a section on "Aims Talk" and later offers an entire chapter aptly titled, "Aims Must Matter." Thornton's curricular aims talk is about the teacher linking broad education aims such as active citizenship in a three-tiered alignment with the (1) course goals of individual classes, (2) individual unit plans, and (3) lesson objectives.

Tending to this structure anoints the teacher the curriculum gatekeeper. Further, just like "history" and "geography" have dual meanings depending on whether they refer to some formal curriculum versus how a student *uses* them in experience, so too do aims. Dewey used the term aim to describe what happens within *an* experience when a person establishes an *aim in light of an end-in-view*.

Thornton argues that the rise of the standards movement beginning in the 1990s subverted aims talk and led to the dubious assumption that education is about maintaining or enhancing our economic prosperity, and the only surefire way of achieving this goal is for students to do well in traditional social science subject areas like history and geography.

In effect, this subversion accelerates a longer-term trend to emasculate teachers' involvement in the process of aims construction and decision making resulting in a serious disconnect between aims and pedagogy. He then reminded us that these broad curricular aims come from three sources: the abilities and interests of our students, societal needs, and from research.

Although Dewey's philosophy supplies the foundation for the social studies, which today is reflected in the standards and position statements of the main professional organization, NCSS, students rarely learn social studies in schools. Teachers are more likely to require that students commit information to short-term memory because of the dominance and prestige of the history discipline, as well as the favored status of content over conceptual learning as evident in many of the curriculum frameworks (Erickson, 2008). Likewise, Barth and Shermis (1970) identified three pedagogical traditions in social studies classrooms that are still valid today, but with some critical differences.

THE THREE PEDAGOGICAL TRADITIONS

The 1970s were a time of intense interest for both the adherents and critics of John Dewey, as well as the soul of the social studies, which perhaps were not unrelated (Stuckart & Glanz, 2010). A resurgence of interest in Dewey following the twentieth anniversary of his death led to a spate of scholarly writings and public debates about his philosophy and the implications for education, including some writers who erroneously alleged that he advocated following the impulses and interests of children wherever they may go (Darling, 1994).

At the start of the decade, the competing doctrines and philosophies of the social studies sparked James Barth and S. Samuel Shermis from Purdue University to publish an article in *Social Education* about the three pedagogical traditions of value, knowledge, and skills integration in the social studies (Barth & Shermis, 1970), and eventually culminated with a book, *The Nature of the Social Studies*, by the end of the decade written with the addition of their colleague, Robert Barr (Barr et al., 1978).

In an exceptionally well-reasoned manner, they presented the three models as Citizenship Transmitter, Social Scientist, and Reflective Inquiry in order from most to least prevalent. The Reflective Inquiry teacher—the rarest of all and the one who implements the Deweyan problem and inquiry approach to learning—has perhaps edged even closer to extinction.

In the intervening four decades since publication, the cultural wars rooted in the 1980s and bitterly fought during the 1990s resulted in a high-stakes testing and accountability regime, which transformed the social scientist approach into the Historian-only Social Scientist position, subverted teacher aims for high-stakes tests, and ultimately strengthened the Citizenship Transmission model.

The Traditional Approach: Citizenship Transmission Teachers

The seeds of the Citizenship Transmission model came from earliest human settlements. Evidence of this approach is found in the Bible, ancient Roman writings, and Chinese texts. By the middle of the nineteenth century, the public school model of Horace Mann emphasized the development of student virtue and character with an added aim of social efficiency (Cubberley, 1947). Today, Citizenship Transmission teachers are the most common type of social studies teachers and the least likely to adopt a social studies approach to learning suggesting they hold rigid belief systems.

These sticky beliefs serve as an influential aims source and emphasize acceptance and conformity to certain values and participation like paying taxes, defending the country, and supporting a certain vision of how America should look and function. Teachers conceive their role as the protagonists, leading students to the right answers. Therefore, they carefully select the content to support their positions, interpret it, and then instruct the students how to feel about it.

This dominant perspective rests on the assumption that students should incorporate these beliefs (i.e., "truths") into their own worldviews. Dewey's admonishment about the nascent social studies curriculum's potential for becoming a source of dogmatism and indoctrination seems prophetic (Dewey, 1946). After more than a century of learning content in this manner, most evidence suggests that in the very least, it has led to the disengagement of young people in our classrooms and in exercising their full citizenship whether it is voting or other forms of participation.

Disciplinary Tools: Social Scientist Approach Teachers

Unlike a Citizenship Transmitter in a social science curriculum arrangement, the Social Scientist teachers bring their validated tools of a social science discipline to the social studies classroom as historians, psychologists, sociologists, anthropologists, and the other specialist areas. Their purpose is to instruct the students to employ these tools to analyze real-world problems through the lens of the discipline's concepts.

An example would be a Social Scientist history class teacher, who having earned an economics degree, models to students how to examine community data sets by income levels to reach conclusions about poverty in a historical context. With the rise of the social sciences in the 1960s and 1970s, foundations and other entities poured money into developing high school curriculum from these individual social science perspectives. One of the more popular programs in the 1970s was called MACOS, Man: A Course of Study, a socio-anthropological approach based on the educational theories of Jerome Bruner (Bruner, 1977).

Today, this is not the case because much of the financial support for the Social Scientist curricula evaporated as the 1980s ushered in a conservative political period with intense interest in perpetuating the Citizenship Transmission model. For example, one of the most provocative books of the time was E. D. Hirsch's *Cultural Literacy: What Every American Needs to Know* (1988) where he castigated Dewey for being too eager to reject essential information and the state of the social studies field being more interested in process than content.

The Social Scientist teacher is more a historical anomaly than a lasting phenomenon because of the 1990s "conservative restoration" and "the revival of history and geography and a return to the disciplines" (Evans, 2004, p. 171). Much like historians won control of the curriculum in the late nineteenth century, today they are the de facto winners despite all the efforts of NCSS and myriad social studies teacher preparation programs to adopt standards requiring candidates' familiarity with concepts derived from the major social sciences and provide guidance for a social studies approach like the Reflective Inquiry model.

Perhaps one way to interpret this turn of events is to view the vicious cultural wars of the 1990s as transforming the Social Scientist into the Historian-only model, which ultimately reinforces the role of the social studies teacher as Citizenship Transmitter. Ironically, In *Where Did the Social Studies Go*

Wrong? (2003), conservative contributors blamed the sorry state of social studies learning and the lack of young voter participation on the liberal university professors and poorly trained teachers.

One of the commentators argued that these teachers failed in their mission of "transmitting to each new generation the political vision of liberty and equality before the law" (Finn Jr., 2003, p. vi). A recurring theme throughout is that teachers are not *transmitting* citizenship enough because they are more concerned with political correctness. They argued for a college-like social science curriculum, which ignores the interests and aptitudes of the young learners while also ignoring the copious data suggesting that is exactly how most instruction is conducted in social studies classrooms.

Further evidence of this Citizenship Transmission dominance is found in the testing realm. Beginning in the early 1970s, the College Board began incorporating document-based questions, DBQs, into the history advanced placement exams. In the 1990s, many states and districts expanded access to advanced placement courses. Some states like New York began creating DBQ history exams as part of their high-stakes testing requirements.

Ironically, the recent rise of the CCS movement should have satisfied both the history camp as well as the Reflective Inquiry one, because as will become evident later, the standards offer a middle position. However, political forces have intervened with strong resistance from groups on both sides of the political spectrum. Conservatives, many of who initially supported the state-led initiatives later rejected them under the banner of federal overreach, while liberals also rejected them because they did not fully consider the needs of teachers and learners.

While we should be celebrating a shift away from a pure multiple-choice testing regime, it is difficult not to lament the fact that the CCS emphasis is often on the *mechanics* of writing and the formulaic teaching to the DBQ essay prompt rather than how a historian critically thinks; the ubiquitous narrowing of the curriculum to pass the high-stakes tests at any cost; and the focus on looking to the past rather than contemporary social issues for the sources of aims (Grant, Gradwell, & Cimbricz, 2004).

For example, compared to Reflective Inquiry teachers, Social Scientist historians tend to be much less concerned about studying the past through today's problems. Further, they mostly restrict their evidence to the historical record rather than expanding out to other social science domains (Barr et al., 1978).

Dewey in Action: Reflective Inquiry Teachers

With a spotlight on student needs, aptitudes, and interests, the least-implemented approach in social studies classrooms over the past century has been the Reflective Inquiry perspective (Barr et al., 1978). Rising shortly after the turn of the twentieth century, Dewey's ideas took hold in a handful of progressive schools, which emphasized community and active occupations. Early examples include The Park School of Baltimore (1912) and the Little Red School House (1921) in New York City (Stuckart & Glanz, 2010).

Reflective Inquiry Teachers truly endeavor to know their individual students including their socioeconomic backgrounds, likes and dislikes, biases and interests. The overriding consideration is to make the students aware of their interests even if the students only faintly perceive them at the time. In other words, the teacher values the experiences of her students and then creates active learning opportunities to engage them in hypothesis testing, analysis, and truth building because all knowledge is tentative.

Despite the obstacles including the testing mandates and the structural barriers of schools like forty-five-minute class periods and textbook-driven resources, some teachers achieve a degree of fidelity to the Reflective Inquiry mode of teaching (Misco & Hamot, 2012). Not only are these teachers well-versed in the content of social studies, but they also are knowledgeable about learning psychology and philosophy.

They are willing to perfect their craft in conducting discussions, provide substantive feedback, and allow their students power and choices in accomplishing learning objectives. The Reflective Inquiry teacher looks to the students, the problems, and challenges in creating a better society and scholarship as the source of aims (Barr et al., 1978).

Given the myriad teacher constraints and limitations, "Reflective teaching is best understood as an ideal aim, which can never be perfectly realized" (Thornton, 1994, p. 10). Teachers can strive to know their students better, improve their skills in facilitating discussions—especially around controversial issues and topics—and design substantive learning experiences requiring the students to collaborate, solve problems, and construct meaning.

DESIGNING AND IMPLEMENTING A REFLECTIVE INQUIRY CURRICULUM

Although Dewey published prolifically, he did not work out many of the details in putting his philosophy into practice, especially considering the complexity of the endeavor across infinite contexts. Instead, he recognized the importance of research and the contributions of others. In broad strokes, though, Dewey articulated learning as beginning with "a *forked-road* situation, a situation which is ambiguous, which presents a dilemma, which proposes alternatives" (*HWT*, p. 11). The learner then inquired within an immediate experience because the process of the activity (i.e., methods) and ends (i.e., learning goals) were part of the same contiguous action.

One way social studies teachers can work toward a Deweyan curriculum is to plan one or more educative learning experiences each marking period incorporating structures like long-term projects, issues-centered units and lessons, thematic and reverse chronology units. These structures support a Deweyan foundation where the teacher is an active partner every step of the way as she cultivates a community of learners, guides the disciplining of student interests; and creates variations of problem-based inquiries.

Beyond the active learning planning phase, the teacher plays an outsized role in leading students to discover and discipline their interests. While it is highly unlikely that a teacher can plan individualized tasks for every student, she can give students choices. Depending on their ages and abilities, the teacher's facilitator role can reach deeply into all phases within each structure. For example, when designing a project for younger children or high-needs students, the teacher may propose topics, direct the fieldwork, scaffold a discussion, stimulate questions, tally ideas, and provide other types of support (O'Brien, 2002).

Likewise, valuing a community of learners suggests that the interaction among students is essential for constructing meaning. Interactions have the potential to be the most powerful when students have an opportunity to associate with others who are different from themselves in all ways including culturally, socioeconomically, and ethnically. This process of learning involves developing a sensitivity and analysis through multiple perspectives and offers an example of how the teacher bridges the formal curriculum and mimics powerful thinking in all realms of our personal experiences, not just when working within the confines of a history problem.

Moreover, these interactions are meant to provide a set of social tools that students develop and use for inquiry, or, as Glassman (2001) explains, "Dewey's solution is to educate the individual and diversify the social milieu so that these tools will be brought into question (a bottom-up/indeterminate approach)" (p. 6). Further, all learning begins with a problem, and all problems require inquiry.

Inquiry can be much more than the most robust form, the scientific method, where an individual hypothesizes, collects data, selects a course of action, and then tests the solution back in experience. Inquiry can also include processes like asking a wiser (i.e., more experienced) person questions, looking back to past experiences, or seeking out other sources. In a sense, a learner is developing, maintaining, and following her interests.

The interests propel the entire process. Teachers are charged with opening students' lives to new possibilities and experiences, which allow them to discover their likes and dislikes, explore their natural aptitudes, stretch their boundaries, and engage in a continuous, virtuous cycle of experiences where deep and sustained learning leads to even more learning, which is the highest aim of education. The educational equivalent for continuous experiences is active occupations (Pring, 2007).

Active Occupations

Echoing the doings and makings of our ancestors, Dewey embraced the idea of active occupations, particularly for younger learners. Dewey's Laboratory School at the University of Chicago featured a curriculum clustered around various occupations. One reported example from fall 1896 describes young elementary students studying the connection between occupations and geography in Holland including building dykes with chairs (Tanner, 1997).

One of the fruitful outcomes was an entire chapter in *The School and Society* (1900) aptly named, "The Psychology of Occupations," where he defined occupations as "a mode of activity on the part of the child which reproduces, or runs parallel to, some form of work carried on in social life" (p. 83). Dewey insisted that occupations embody the harmony between the mental and physical phases of experience.

Why did active occupations become such a central feature of his curriculum theory? At about the turn of the nineteenth century, the two mainstream curriculum theories included one that was based on following the interests of the child; and the other, on the importance of disciplines of knowledge, meaning that each discipline had its own set of tools, perspectives, and ways of viewing phenomena.

Deweyan pragmatism again offers a middle position, and indeed, Dewey joined the interests of the child with the intellectualized nature of the curriculum. Further, he adopted the idea first posited by the Enlightenment philosopher Johan Friedrich Herbart that the development of the individual mirrors the development of the human race. Therefore, the history curriculum in the Laboratory School primarily followed a linear, chronological organization (Kliebard, 2006).

Dewey continued to flesh out many of the details in chapter 15 of *Democracy and Education* (1916), "Play and Work in the Curriculum." Beginning with the premise that young students should learn similarly to work and play in the wider society, Dewey advocated that teachers begin with individual student's "native tendencies" (p. 147). Because all knowledge is ultimately social in nature, Dewey believed that active social occupations like gardening, painting, cooking, drawing, and singing could transform into powerful forces leading students to become naturally inquisitive.

Dewey cited five reasons: (1) it requires the student use all her senses; (2) it addresses and parallels human needs based on a social production, exchange, and consumption model; (3) it is free from the association of doing something merely for pecuniary gain; (4) it becomes a self-propelling enterprise as the

Table 2.1. Characteristics, Pros, and Cons of Curriculum Structures to Support a Deweyan Approach to Learning Social Studies

Curriculum Structure	Emphasized Characteristics	Pros	Cons
Long-Term Projects	Teacher facilitates conditions for students to immerse themselves in activities, discover their interests and question topics, set their own goals, and then drive the inquiry (Glassman, 2001) Authentic Intellectual Work (AIW) involves knowledge construction, disciplined inquiry, and value beyond school (Newmann, Bryk, & Nagaoka, 2001)	Potential for broad focus on the curriculum Cognitive autonomy as the learner relates learning tasks to own experiences (Taba, 1963) Large-scale studies support student learning and growth (Smith, Lee, & Newmann, 2001)	Time consuming to plan and facilitate May become unwieldy and unmanageable AIW focuses less on discovery learning and more on disciplined inquiry May disrupt teacher curriculum pacing
Thematic Units	Theme originates in a problem or societal challenge (Misco, 2014)	Interdisciplinary Concept-focused (Erickson, 2008)	Time consuming to plan and facilitate May disrupt teacher curriculum pacing
Issues-Centered Lessons	Approach emphasizes societal problem-solving with a focus on common needs and student interests, and an interdisciplinary approach to devising solutions (Wraga, 1999)	Can lead to democratic deliberation and discourse Student-selected controversial issues heighten interest	Teachers avoid controversial public issues Many teachers lack the skills to conduct effective discussions (Hess, 2010) May disrupt teacher curriculum pacing
Reverse Chronology Units	Teachers and students select issues and ideas for exploration and then look to past epochs for explanation and knowledge-building (Misco & Patterson, 2009)	Integrative and interdisciplinary Springboard for more ideas and controversial issues integration	Time consuming to plan and facilitate May disrupt teacher curriculum pacing

Note. All the approaches are student-centered beginning with problems leading to hypothesis-building, inquiry, diverse perspectives, experimentation, student judgments, and shared knowledge-building.

student pursues related and wider areas of inquiry; and (5) social occupations provide the impetus and materials for the creation of the sciences (*DE*). Ultimately, though, active occupations can only be effective when embedded within a Deweyan-friendly curriculum structure.

Curriculum Structures

Dewey supplied a philosophical framework and descriptive theoretical underpinnings, but he also recognized that it was up to others to work out the details and conduct research into how things worked in various conditions. One of the challenges of the social studies field is that there have been very few formal, large-scale, classroom studies.

One of the most recent ones (John Saye & Social Studies Inquiry Research Collaborative (SSIRC), 2013) reconstituted a design based on another from about thirty years ago, where a team of researchers focused on the correlation between authentic intellectual work (AIW) and standardized test scores in a variety of Chicago elementary schools (Newmann, Bryk, & Nagaoka, 2001; Scheurman & Newmann, 1998). Before that, we would probably have to turn to John Goodlad's seminal research from the early 1980s, which he reported in *A Place Called School* (1984).

The SSIRC group's findings mainly confirmed the lack of Deweyan rigor in social studies classrooms, which also reaffirmed Goodlad's assessment that the social studies is still taught as a process of dates, names, and memorization. Some of the findings in these rare and comprehensive studies help illuminate Dewey's theories suggesting that students who are empowered with classroom control and choices, and can frequently engage in inquiry while studying problems and issues relevant to their lives, are motivated learners who score higher on standardized assessments.

From the social studies teacher's perspective, implementing structures to support this type of learning are daunting, and may involve great risk to new teachers whose salary and tenure decisions may hinge on student test scores. Veteran teachers also face risks as school officials may deny them precious resources, or they become demoralized from being labeled an ineffective teacher.

The complexities of teaching and external mandates favor a more traditional approach as teachers navigate the broad scope of the curriculum in short, standard time periods, prepare students for high-stakes tests, differentiate instruction for inclusive classrooms, and all the other things necessary for successfully managing a classroom. The list of requirements keeps growing as we become more obsessed with collecting data (often flawed), and then requiring teachers to act on the data and document the effects.

Therefore, it is not surprising that most teachers fail to implement "A Vision of Powerful Teaching and learning in the Social Studies" (National

Council for the Social Studies, 2016). In the final analysis, it is a highly risky, cognitively demanding, time-consuming enterprise. A pragmatic approach could be to challenge teacher candidates to experiment, take risks, and start small if necessary by gradually integrating projects, thematic units, issues-centered units and lesson plans, and perhaps designing an entire course using a reverse chronology approach (see table 2.1).

Long-Term Projects

Projects can mean many things to many people. In fact, one joy of being a social studies teacher is that the boundless curriculum allows infinite opportunities for creative tasks. From a Deweyan perspective, AIW is a powerful example backed up by the research. We can begin with the simple notion that a project is a curriculum arrangement that allows students to study some event, topic, or phenomenon in some depth and over an extended period.

When defining AIW, the researchers defined high-quality work by the three essential attributes: construction of knowledge, disciplined inquiry, and value beyond school. AIW reflects the work adults do to function in a modern society. In many jobs, they are expected to solve problems by constructing knowledge or forming a novel solution. For the solutions to be sufficient, adults must acquire a foundation of basic skills and disciplinary knowledge.

Further, the ability to use that knowledge to promote deep understanding is a characteristic of disciplined inquiry. In occupations, adults normally engage in elaborated communication, and in concert, report the outcomes. In sum, AIW envisions that when adults work, they draw on a prior knowledge base in a specific field, they apply that knowledge base in unique ways to promote deep understanding on specific tasks, and they use complex communication both during the process and at the conclusion to apply the findings.

Thematic Units

When designing thematic units, social studies teachers should carefully consider a theme originating in a problem or societal challenge (Misco, 2014). Further, this type of unit may help facilitate collaboration among teachers across or within disciplines to assist students in reaching some deeper understandings about the theme. When two 10th grade U.S. history teachers constructed a thematic unit around the concept of war, they successfully integrated simulations, discussions, and critical thinking.

However, as the unit progressed along an eight-week timeline, the teachers gradually reverted to a traditional, transmission model of teaching. The researchers concluded that rigid teacher beliefs about how social studies should be taught contributed to the final outcome (Anderson & Cook, 2014).

This example also reaffirms the tricky nature of beliefs and the strong tug social studies teachers experience to return to the traditional teaching fold.

Issues-Centered Units and Lessons

A cornerstone of Dewey's curriculum theory is social progress—a forward-looking perspective where the moral adjudication of social problems enhances the prospects for all individuals—is also embedded in the NCSS Position Statement about powerful teaching and learning. NCSS calls for a curriculum focused "on pervasive and enduring social issues" with students considering solutions and the consequences of those solutions (National Council for the Social Studies, 2016, p. 181).

Teachers plan issues-centered instruction around complex social problems defined as those issues that lead to disagreements among knowledgeable and informed individuals. Further, teachers can utilize a range of structures from inter- to intra-disciplinary contexts with unlimited ways building structures within the range. For example, some teachers may consider limiting the number of questions while others may place an emphasis on the level of controversy a topic elicits (Caron, 2004).

Reverse Chronology Units

The idea of designing a history curriculum starting with the present is an old idea. While advocating a reverse chronology approach to the curriculum, Finch (1942) described his successes and challenges with implementing a European history course beginning with current events and working backwards in time to the Middle Ages. He justified the arrangement because the material was most familiar to the students' experiences and current events sparked greater interest than distant history.

He suggested that the approach also supported small research projects and led to students grasping causal relationships more effectively than in a traditional curricular arrangement. Ever more surprising, "An unexpected outcome was finding that the importance of some of mankind's fundamental beliefs which have influenced people through the centuries became apparent of themselves after several units" (p. 365). In other words, he alleged that students could inductively discover what we might call "Big ideas" today.

Misco (2014) recently summarized the approach in Deweyan, NCSS best practices terms when he described the reverse chronology unit as beginning with *problems* rooted in the present. Social studies students would then enhance their young experiences "through an active inquiry into the antecedents, causes and explanations of the present" (p. 245). It is only in present existential conditions, of course, that one can have an experience and thus establishing a personal connection to a problematic situation.

Table 2.2. The Social Studies Curriculum Continuum

	Subject Matter	Teacher	Learner
More General ↕ **More Specific**	Other people's experiences	Psychologizes the curriculum	Instruments for enlarging the learner's experience
	Formulated, logically organized subject matter and materials of instruction	Curriculum expert	Subject matter and methods are unified within an experience
	Social studies as unlimited subject matter	Curriculum gatekeeper (Thornton, 2005)	Enlarging an experience begins with a social study
	All school subject matter as facts and concepts	Reflective Inquiry social studies teachers develop a level of mastery across all subject areas, an understanding of how young people learn, and clear communication with individual learners to foster inquiry communities based on interests, needs, and aptitudes They also re-conceptualize the curriculum using unit aims as they maintain fidelity to the abstract and theoretical underpinnings of the subject matter (Barr, Barth, & Shermis, 1978; Pring, 2007; Thornton, 2005)	Subject matter's instrumentality to become events within an experience
	History as facts and principles of the past		History's instrumentality to allow learner to see the human connections of an ordinary act in the present
	Geography as facts and principles		Geography's instrumentality to allow learner to see the spatial connections of an ordinary act
	Science as facts and principles		Science's instrumentality as final, settled knowledge because of deliberate observation, reflection, and testing; states meanings
	Math as facts, principles, and propositions with the removal of all existential material		Math's instrumentality to regulate the relationship of consequences to ends within an experience
	Language as facts and principles		Language's instrumentality to provide meaning and significance to events and consequences; inner experience finds meaning in social milieu
	Art as facts, concepts, and products		Art's instrumentality to express meaning; it is the aesthetic, rhythmic force that finds order as it consummates an experience

Note. Dewey described the curriculum as the learner and subject matter along the same continuum. Because school subject matter has already been subjected to intelligence, the curriculum becomes a directional force unifying subject matter and methods within *an* experience.

THE SOCIAL STUDIES CURRICULUM CONTINUUM

To the pragmatist, the cherished aim of education is for students to become aware that all beliefs are tentative, based on the current best knowledge available, but subject to reform with new facts and concepts. With critical reflection, students can grow and develop the tools, knowledge, and habits to effectively resolve problems, but they can never achieve a final and complete perfection. Framed within his naturalism, Dewey described a curriculum theory where subject matter and methods unify within a person's experience.

Dewey famously declared, "The child and the curriculum are simply two limits which define a single process" (*CC*, p. 109), something we might call the learning process today (see table 2.2). Dewey's insistence on unification belies his beliefs of the continuous nature of experience; the ability of an individual to discover and reconstruct the connections; and finally, the resulting elimination of philosophical dualisms of "matter and mind" within the experience itself (*DE*, p. 210). Therefore, how does curriculum enlarge a student's experience?

Using the Curriculum to Enlarge an Experience

It is easy to imagine a scenario where a teacher decides to implement a thematic unit on the topic of slavery and the Columbian Exchange. Earlier, several students talked about how their families had traced ancestors to slavery and others interjected how they were surprised that when they studied the Roman Republic, some slaves served as accountants and medical doctors.

After the teacher poses a question about human rights, one student mentions he watched a video about human trafficking and contemporary slavery. As the conversation continues, the room buzzes with excitement as more and more of his peers start making connections between human rights and slavery today.

By giving the students choices and skillfully conducting a discussion to help them identify their interests, the teacher is psychologizing the curriculum. She also considers every student's capacities and needs as she assigns them to groups, provides enrichment materials, and guides them to pursue deep dives into the subject matter.

The teacher assigns the students to small cooperative learning groups with specific roles, and then provides them with resources: print materials, an information sheet with links to electronic items, recording and planning documents, laptop computers, and a performance assessment requiring each student develop a human rights action plan. The entire endeavor focuses around the question, "In what ways do the conditions and consequences of modern slavery differ and mirror the Atlantic slave trade during the Columbian exchange?"

Ultimately, the students will choose how they will advance human rights, but they must be able to demonstrate a historical understanding of slavery to make their case by providing a context statement addressing the political, economic, social, and ideological dimensions of slavery now and then. The teacher crafts the question based on student interests and because it offers a rich opportunity to incorporate many elements of her district's global history curriculum.

From an individual student's perspective, the activity is a potentially rich source as well to enlarge her experiences. Although she learned about the triangular trade the previous week and completed short answer questions as part of an earlier assignment, she did not reflect on how slavery today is alike and different from certain points in history. Confronted with this unique problem, she cannot rely on habit to arrive at an acceptable solution. First, she feels overwhelmed with the enormity of the task. But soon, she musters courage, and begins to engage with her partners. All human endeavors are colored *with emotions*.

After the activity, the student commences a context statement. The immediate *object of inquiry* is to compare the political dimensions. She examines a contemporary world map showing the estimated percentage of each country's population subjugated to slavery and notices that the United States, Canada, and the countries of Western Europe are the places least likely to hold humans in bondage.

She thinks back to what she previously learned about the governments of Western Europe and the United States and concludes that the places with the least modern slavery are democracies. She recalls that in her previous social studies class the year before, she color-coded a world map based on the relative strength of democracy. In other words, she is connecting her thinking and *doing geography*.

At the same time, she is recalling *an event* in her thinking (equivalent to any recall such as solving a math problem with the value of pi). She is *doing history* as she begins to make connections to her prior knowledge. She is also *doing math* as she suspends thinking about individual countries and instead perceives patterns based on democratic forms of government. She shares her finding with her partners.

As the object of her inquiry proceeds, she tests her theory back in primary experience or put another way, she is *doing science* by considering the consequences. She studies the map and notices that one of the highest concentrations of modern slavery is in India. A partner remarks that India is also a democracy. The teacher, who is observing, approaches the group. She directs them to an article on slavery in India. A vigorous give-and-take among the group members ensues as they begin to shape a nuanced view based on historical and cultural factors. The give-and-take is *doing English*—using language to make meaning socially and culturally with others.

The student returns to crafting her response, and a feeling of satisfaction washes over her as she finishes. The coming together of loose ends into a settled state is *doing art*. However, the settled state is only a temporary destination because it serves as the launch for the next experience. In this illustration, one could substitute our ancestors trying to solve the problem of how to avoid a hungry lion, and the expanding of the experience is the same because our forebears still used geography, history, math, science, language and art, which is the uniquely human process of intelligence.

SUMMARY

You cannot have a social study without history and geography, as well as the social sciences and humanities. Although the problem is often framed as a choice between social studies and history approaches in a Deweyan best practice, they interpenetrate each other. Human participation in nature's rhythms means that every existence has a history, with some beginning, middle, and end. In addition to the temporal aspect, every history also has a geographic location where it takes place. Therefore, all historical events consist of unique individual interactions and unduplicated situations.

What one might today refer to as the formal, history and geography curricula include all those past events, locations, and peoples deemed important in *present* studies. Moreover, it is also about how one *uses* history because "our ancestors were intelligent; they took their errors, mistakes, biases, and prejudices and systematically ordered them so that they might be more easily learned" (Austin, 1965, p. 202). The process of abstracting other people's past experiences into our own individual experiences means that subject matter is more than just other people's experiences, it becomes a means or moving force in active thinking and inquiry.

History transforms into a regulatory force because thinking is "a step in the reconstruction of temporal order in human experience" (Blau, 1960, p. 94), the reason that Dewey wrote about history more than any other subject area. Most of the common names we give to curriculum like math, science, and history take on a double meaning when described in other people's past experiences versus an active individual's thinking, especially in the context of formal schooling.

A vision for social studies teachers demands that teachers reflect and acknowledge their beliefs toward the subject matter, how students learn, and the nature of knowledge. The teacher's job is not to indoctrinate students to one point of view. In addition, the process does not have to result in a zero-sum game where either a conservative or liberal political disposition determines the teaching strategies and learning experiences. By creating a curriculum structure where students have opportunities to study current problems to strengthen democracy, teachers leave the door open for students to explore their own political proclivities, and to form judgments grounded in reasons and evidence and subject to review by one's peers.

More importantly, the process mirrors the way that our ancestors survived in the world. What modern humans label history, geography, math, science, and other content areas originated in humans who were solving everyday problems. What eventually emerges as "subject matter" is merely a term denoting other people's areas of knowledge derived from the past.

The teacher assumes the crucial role of taking the curriculum and connecting it to the student's everyday experiences. At the same time, subject matter has the potential to become objects for enlarging a learner's experiences. Fundamentally, the social studies teacher facilitates the instrumentality of the curriculum, which has the potential to lead to *an* experience, the subject of chapter 3.

Chapter 3

Experience

Focus Questions:

1 Why did Dewey place such great importance on the denotative method?
2 What are the characteristics of an educative social studies experience?
3 What is the logical foundation of history education as instrumental?

The last chapter ended with the suggestion for social studies teachers to plan some type of long-term project or curriculum structure that supported active, collaborative learning. Now, it is time to expand the rationale for these curriculum arrangements. And because this concerns value and the nature of knowledge, the discussion is necessarily a philosophical activity. The anchor is Dewey's theory of experience, which is central in his system of ideas.

This chapter begins with the rationale for why Dewey embraced a theory of experience as congruent with nature. Equally important, it proceeds to distinguish what it means to have *an* experience and how education is a way to shortcut the process. Further, it addresses the failure of individuals to form beliefs based on intelligent thinking, which Dewey viewed as the greatest threat to democracy, social relations, and material progress.

Next, the chapter presents the characteristics of educative experiences for the social studies and the formation of moral and historical judgments in experience. And finally, because human history and geography are the principle elements in experience, a discussion ensues about how the instrumental purpose of history education is to socialize young people. *Consequently, a goal for social studies teachers is to identify the experiences the students bring to school, and then bridge the gap between them and the curriculum to promote instrumental, cognitive activity.*

EXPERIENCE AND THE NATURAL WORLD

According to Dewey, the greatest hindrance to human progress is the inability or unwillingness of people to use intelligence to form their beliefs. Before pragmatism emerged in the middle of the nineteenth century, earlier philosophical systems overcame insuperable, logical dualism roadblocks with appeals to a higher being or to some overarching Reason. Dewey adopted a basic unit of analysis, experience, based on the work of earlier pragmatists like William James. Experience became a theory that fit the evidence of a world based on physics and natural phenomena including social relations.

Dewey defined experience as the *interaction* of a person's needs, desires, purposes, and abilities with the objective circumstances of the surrounding environment. The product of an interaction is a *situation*. The subject matter of experience involves human history and geography because all situations have spatial-temporal characteristics. Further, education is a way to shortcut experience in the wider world outside of schools where teachers create situations with *educative experiences* for young people to learn adult organizations of information.

Having *an* Experience

Darwin explicated how every living organism co-evolved with the environment. Dewey labeled the relationship "a transaction" and explained further, "An organism does not live in an environment; it lives by means of an environment" (*LTI*, p. 32). As the highest form of life, only humans have the capacity to experience the environing conditions, and employ intelligence to address perceived problems.

When an individual encounters obstacles, conflict, or resistance, she colors her experience with feelings and ideas as purpose emerges. Most of the time, the experience remains crude and undeveloped, and never becomes *an* experience, a full-fledged affair with a beginning, middle, and end. Perhaps she experiences dissonance between what she feels, thinks, and observes, or she becomes distracted from her original purpose.

She searched for her keys, hears a sudden sound, and then forgets what she is doing. The experience ends, not because it has run its natural course to fulfillment, but because of some external distraction or internal deviation. She encounters a boss who chastises her when he perceives her work as insufficient, and she shuts down. She descends into a rut and habitually drifts through her day. She plays video games and develops a slack attitude, which stifles the next experience. Perhaps she shifts among experiences so wantonly that she emerges harried and scatterbrained. These are mis-educative experiences and they retard her from controlling future ones.

Most of the ways a person experiences the world is non cognitive. The beginning of any type of experience is her crude brush with things or as Dewey puts it, "Something had and enjoyed" (*EN*, p 84). She cringes at the sound of a loud noise, or follows a morning habit of brushing her teeth, or enjoys a quiet walk along a nature trail, but these activities involve minimal or no cognition. There is no middle or end. The experiences stop abruptly as when a shining light diverts her gaze.

In contrast, when one has *an* experience, she considers the challenge, and then works out the next steps to achieve some desired goal. As she proceeds toward the goal, she constantly adjusts and adapts to changing conditions all the while keeping the end in view. Unlike most of her experiences, which either end abruptly or never build steam, *an* experience transcends the crude and inchoate and forms a continuous chain in her life's journey. The experience leads to satisfaction, consummation, a rounding of a situation to complete fulfillment. The same impulses that lead to a satisfactory conclusion also drive the production of knowledge and nourish interest for the next full experience.

Perhaps she solves a math problem, paints a fence, composes an essay, participates in a tennis match, enjoys a satisfying meal, or debates the fine points of a trade agreement and comparative advantage. These complete experiences are imbued with their own original and unique qualities and provide the fodder for further experiences, not hard stops. Every experience is its own history with distinct plots, rhythms, beginnings, and ends. It is also a forward march in time.

In *Experience and Nature* (1929), Dewey called activity that was non-cognitive or minimally cognitive "primary experience." Primary experience supplies the materials for reflective activity in "secondary experience," and includes things experienced in isolation (i.e., devoid of reflection) that can be merely *had*, *enjoyed*, or *used*. Further, non instrumental and non cognitive activity is immediate and felt, like how one senses pleasure after smelling fragrant flowers or recoiling after grabbing the handle of a hot pan.

Primary experience also includes a phase of activity that is non instrumental and minimally cognitive, something Dewey and other pragmatists struggled to describe (Hickman, 2001). Possible examples comprise a snap decision to turn left at the fork in a road or selecting a type of breakfast cereal among the same variety with only a fleeting consideration. In short, the defining characteristics of the two phases of primary experience are activities that are more immediate than reflective, and their critical role in supplying the crude materials for reflection in secondary experience.

During secondary experience, a person relates the isolated details of similar activities in primary experience with things known leading to a form of controlled, systematic thinking about the activity. For example, a student who enjoys reading about the French Revolution constructs meaning after she reflects on how it relates to similar events such as the American Revolution. The relational process of abstraction, in turn, creates the *objects* of importance for secondary experience.

The two phases of activity in secondary experience are instrumental, meaning they can enlarge a learner's experiences. Most secondary experience is instrumental and *habitual*, making it also non cognitive like primary experience. Without the formation of habits, complex tasks would consume most people's waking hours. For example, after a child learns to ride a bicycle, she does not have to problem-solve every time she wants to ride again. After she masters the ability to balance and produce forward momentum with a pedaling motion, she habitually follows the same pattern thereafter in each subsequent situation.

The most rigorous phase of secondary experience is instrumental and inferential. As the highest form of cognition, this process is also science in the purest form. The inquiry process guides the individual to compare cases derived from primary experience, form a hypothesis, test the hypothesis by making observations and collecting data, and then arriving at a settled belief. She then tests and verifies the belief in the everyday activities of primary experience, which Dewey called "the denotative method" (see figure 3.1).

The Denotative Method: Evolution versus Intelligent Design

Why did Dewey assert the importance of the denotative method? Dewey claimed the denotative method was congruent with experience pertaining to the social world and scientific principles. Despite the significant material advances since the Scientific Revolution, he believed that many individuals clung to erroneous beliefs despite contradictory scientific evidence, which in turn, held society back from greater progress and improved social relations.

He illustrated the role of primary experience as the testing and verification arena for the scientific hypotheses created in secondary experience using the example of Darwin's discoveries, which exploded onto the scene in the middle of the nineteenth century and rocked the foundations of many people's belief systems (*EN*). Although the publication of the *Origin of Species*

Crude Materials	Primary Experience		Verification and Testing
	Noninstrumental	Noncognitive	
	Noninstrumental	Minimally Cognitive	
	Secondary Experience		
	Instrumental/Habitual	Noncognitive	
	Instrumental/Inferential	Cognitive	

Figure 3.1. The Phases of Experience

occurred over 150 years ago, the controversy never abated giving credence to the enduring and pervasive power of customs, beliefs, and attitudes.

Dewey justified his synthesis of a pragmatic philosophy precisely because of these conditions as he aligned observations, principles, and conclusions with the natural world. He contrasted his empirical philosophy with the nonempirical ones that had dominated throughout history. At least since the Middle Ages, creationism or the idea that a supernatural force or God was responsible for the origins of everything that existed held great sway over many peoples. The Judeo-Christian version that gained adherence in the United States was taught as scientific truth in many science and history classrooms based on a strict and literal reading of the Book of Genesis.

In 1987, the Supreme Court of the United States ruled that the teaching of creationism in public schools was a violation of the Establishment Clause of the First Amendment because it disregarded the separation of church and state. Shortly thereafter, the proponents of creationism rebranded their campaign as Intelligent Design, and based it on claims of empirical data, which again rejected the theory of evolution.

The gist of the argument is that some phenomena are so complex that they can only be explained with the existence of an intelligent designer, a supernatural force, a God. Although private and religious schools are free to teach the intelligent design theory of origination, the court system struck down the arguments for inclusion in public curriculum.

Scientific Principles

A clear and overwhelming majority of scientists today support evolution and do not view intelligent design as a theory based on scientific principles because of an absence of empirical evidence. In common discourse, people often substitute theory with hypothesis, but in science, a theory is a conclusion reached after rigorous observation, evidence, and testing. A robust theory fits the facts of the natural world and predicts future consequences. For example, the theory of gravity is a well-established phenomenon to explain the attraction forces between two objects, and few expect the emergence of competing theories given the weight and depth of the evidence.

Scientists acknowledge theories to be tentative and open to empirical testing, and when conflicting evidence materializes, they modify or refine them. They also subject theories to multiple, controlled observations and verify that they operate in a consistent manner. Likewise, they construct theories following the law of parsimony, meaning they conceive them with the fewest and clearest assumptions. And lastly, they ensure that the theories serve a useful function with a direct connection to observation and predictability (National Academy of Sciences Institute of Medicine, 2008; Quammen, 2004).

Evolution survived as a robust theory for over 150 years because of the denotative method. Darwin and a handful of others reached similar conclusions at about the same time, and afterwards, legions of scientists tested these ideas with further evidence despite the widespread criticism and skepticism of the nineteenth-century scientific community. Most of these experimenters held mainstream religious beliefs, and they did not perceive their beliefs in conflict with evolution and natural selection.

The real problem in the evolution versus creationism debate is members of the public fail to use science—the highest form of intelligence—to reach their own conclusions, which results in beliefs and attitudes contrary to the best, available evidence. This state of affairs has left wide swathes of the public vulnerable to disinformation and dogmatism, which Dewey recognized as the greatest threat to democracy and prosperity.

The major challenge for social studies teachers has never been about whether young people vote or "learn" the hallowed history about the United States and democratic principles, but rather that too many citizens fail to use intelligence to arrive at their own settled conclusions. Even today, the chasm is wide between what the scientific experts believe and members of the public profess about persistent social issues.

The Public and Its Social Beliefs

Over the past several decades, the Pew Research Center has conducted periodic surveys measuring beliefs about science and social issues including evolution. What remains consistent over time is that across a wide range of issues members of the public hold divergent beliefs from the scientific community.

For example, while 98 percent of the scientists unequivocally support an evolutionary theory of living organisms in the latest iteration of the poll, roughly one-third of the population believes in evolution, another one-third admits in a combination of evolution and divine intervention, and the last one-third holds that a Creator formed all living things at some designated time in the past and those things remain unchanged, suggesting species do not evolve over time.

Scientists and members of the public hold even greater divergent beliefs over the safety of genetically modified foods with the scientists agreeing 88 percent of the time, to the public 37 percent, representing a 51-point gap. Similarly, 87 percent of the scientists conclude that climate change is a result of human activity with only 50 percent of the public agreeing with the statement in a 37-point difference. Not surprisingly then, 84 percent of the scientists reported that the public's lack of knowledge about science is a major problem while 14 percent agreed it is a minor one, but a problem nonetheless (Funk & Rainie, 2015).

Many citizens dismiss the denotative method of testing theory in everyday activities, which is what scientists do to verify and report their findings. Instead, many lay people cling to their beliefs, values, and attitudes about social issues. Citizens may believe something is true because they value something else such as a certain religious or political world view that blinds them to the science and consequences in the natural world, which in recent times spawned a new term "fake news" for the empirical data deniers.

The intersection of belief, value, and personal interest can lead to the expression of strong attitudes regarding a social phenomenon. For example, despite a preponderance of evidence suggesting humans are the main cause of climate change, they may seek out the minority scientific opinion without examining and weighing the evidence to affirm their values, and hence bolster their beliefs. Dewey never deviated from his contention that only through immediate experience can the exercise of intelligence address problems and challenges, which is also the charge of teachers in creating educative experiences.

DEWEY, EXPERIENCE, AND EDUCATION

Perhaps it is not surprising that experience is the pillar of Dewey's philosophy given that he named many of his major works with titles like *Experience and Nature* (1929), *Art as Experience* (1934), and *Experience and Education* (1938). All these manuscripts originated in his naturalism phase in the last period of his life after he had an opportunity to work out some of the finer points and amend some major concepts.

Experience and Education (1938) is much more than a refinement and recapitulation of the major points in *Democracy and Education* (1916) because one of the subtexts is also about how progressive educators botched the implementation of many of his ideas by allowing the interests of the child to run roughshod. Dewey spent considerable energy defending his philosophy when teachers abrogated their responsibilities in helping students discipline their interests. Further, what was remarkable about these works was how influential they would become in myriad ways in education; yet today, the connection to Dewey seems lost.

When one thinks about classroom management, she or he probably does not think about Dewey. Yet, one of the major reasons that he devoted the mass of his writings to education is precisely because the experiences of young people were not respected in the schools. Teachers cajoled students to memorize long lists of items, and then forced the students to drudgingly recite them. In this traditional education format, the teacher served as transmitter and disciplinarian.

Dewey was one of the first to recognize that if you respected the experiences and interests of the child, the teacher transforms from authoritarian adversary to a partner and facilitator. An accepted theory of classroom management today is if a teacher plans appropriate activities, the students will be interested, and thus engaged in their work. Effective planning and implementation also reduces opportunities for confusion and disruption.

Likewise, thinking of the social studies classroom as a *situation* focusing on the transactions of students with each other, the teacher, and the surrounding environment makes the planning process more holistic. Too often in education, dualisms serve as the organizing schema beginning at the universities with "curriculum and instruction" and filtering down the education chain to include "practice and pedagogy," "content and method," and "child and curriculum."

Additionally, perceiving the classroom as a situation would also illuminate the contentious issue of depth versus coverage in the social studies curriculum because, held against the backdrop of Dewey's philosophy, coverage implies an absence of interaction between the student and curriculum. A situation, moreover, consists of *educative experiences*—a process, which is also the critical attribute of a democratic society.

Educative Experiences

In Dewey's instrumentalism, education is really a shortcut for experience. In modern society, citizens require that young people attend an artificial, mandatory assembly of other young people where experienced adults construct educative learning experiences to promote adaptation and more growth. Before the emergence of the modern school system, individuals interacted with other people who were also trying to understand their own experiences within a clan or tribe, and later within more formal communities such as religious institutions.

The essential elements of this process of meaning-making can be described as a community of persons, so both the individual and the other community members are changing together, adapting, and growing because of these interactions. To operate ethically or in a moral way means that members respect others' interests as they pursued their own. By addressing the problems within the community, the community enhances the environment for more personal growth. In the widest possible way, *educative experiences are those that provide the potential for further, uninterrupted experiences and more growth.*

Therefore, Dewey defined experience as the *interaction* of an individual's intent, desires, abilities, and wants with the objective conditions of the environment, which also includes the experiences of others like those found in the social studies curriculum. As mentioned earlier, the interaction forms a *situation*. The enlarging of experience (or more succinctly, the building up of more and better experiences where each earlier one informs the next) with adaptation, growth, and reconstruction of the self in the context of a problematic society forms the *longitudinal* aspect of experience while the interaction forms the *lateral* one (*EE*).

Why is this terminology important? By framing an experience within a situation, Dewey dissolved the philosophical dualism trap. The conceptual language captures both the mental processes when a person interprets a *stimulus* and the *reaction* of the surrounding environment, which also suggests three implications. First, one can substitute the words "stimulus and reaction," with "content and method," "child and curriculum," "history and social studies" or something similar delimiting the boundaries of *an* experience.

Second, depending on the context of the experience, method can transform into content and vice versa just like an organism reacts to a stimulus in one instance, and in the next, stimulates the environment. And third, another reason (of many that are presented throughout this book) that Dewey is so sorely misunderstood, is that he could never quite extricate himself from the language of mental operations like "interpret" and "mind." The terms are problematic because they suggest an inner world divorced from the outer, which is exactly the opposite of what he was trying to say. The goal of education is to construct quality experiences.

Education is a way to shortcut experience because young people make their way in the world using adult information and skills (i.e., the curriculum), which socializes them into the complex, modern world. Schools become fabricated, miniature societies serving a vital social purpose. That is why the teacher psychologizes the curriculum based on purposes, desires, wants, and especially abilities. At the same time, the teacher takes into consideration every child's interests.

Characteristics of Educative Social Studies Experiences

Educative experiences embody at least seven specific qualities. First, they must originate in the everyday experiences of living. Young elementary children in social studies classrooms learn about themselves, their families, and social connections long before they master economic concepts like supply and demand. Second, all learning begins with hesitation, doubt, a bump in the road, an uneasy feeling, confusion, or misunderstanding, meaning the selection of problems grows out of present conditions. For example, a young child may wonder why some families look and act different from her own. The problem becomes the spark that ignites inquiry.

Third, the teacher selects the materials from the unbounded social studies curriculum and beyond including the humanities, arts, and sciences. The materials set the problems with the intention of leading to more problems. In other words, the teacher creates a long-term plan to promote longitudinal experiences for her students perpetuating a virtuous cycle of doubt-inquiry-doubt. After completing an investigation about different types of families, the students may develop questions about the roles of different family members like grandparents. The situation leads to an active quest for more information and the production of new and more complex ideas.

Fourth, the production of knowledge is science. When students observe current conditions, reflect in secondary experience forming hypotheses, and then test these hypotheses back in primary experience (i.e., the denotative method), they enlarge these experiences using induction and deduction. Science in experience leads to higher levels of organization in thinking (e.g., concepts, abstractions, generalizations, etc.) just like it historically produces advances in medicine, manufacturing, and production in the physical world.

Fifth, inquiry as science means that truth and knowledge are tentative. Dewey and modern science rests on the assumption that nothing serves as an absolute truth or fixed surety. Active occupations and mechanical skills allow students to select means and ends, and then to consider the consequences. When critics attack the social studies as placing too much importance on skills at the expense of learning content, they fail to recognize that skills are the connectors leading to a continuity of educative, longitudinal experiences. In other words, skills are required to assess truth claims.

Sixth, Dewey's critics fail to grasp that he is not denigrating the importance of learning specific content. The process of learning with skills and active occupations involves an expansion to subject matter, information, ideas, and facts. A young student embarks on a digital history project to interview members of a family about their backgrounds and roles, and in the process, learns about food, culture, and other specific social studies content.

And seventh, the secondary experience of reflection, review, and generalization means that the learner is looking back at previous experiences, extracting what is valuable, and then projecting into the future. Dewey believed that the mind could discover the means-ends relationships. A social studies equivalent *in experience* is the student "doing history," which will be addressed in greater detail in chapter 5.

Psychologizing the Social Studies Curriculum with Experience

The goal of the social studies teacher is to bridge the students' experiences with the adult organizations of information in a unique, boundless curriculum. The starting point is for the teacher to become familiar with her students' interests and experiences. And because the highest aim of education is to promote more growth, in experience terms that means the students should engage in more reflective, inferential activity. Dewey was very clear that primary experience supplies the materials for more intense engagement in secondary experience, and that effective teachers respect and investigate their students' backgrounds.

Since the 1960s, the social studies education field recognizes the importance of valuing the diverse experiences learners bring to the classroom. Advocacy groups and branches of scholarship emerged directly related to Dewey's conception of democracy, which values inclusion and freedom. Housed under the umbrella of social justice, areas like multicultural education and culturally relevant pedagogy become integrated into a vision of good teaching. Over time, the population in the United States has trended to a more diverse and pluralistic composition while many minority groups within schools and society continue to be underserved and underrepresented.

McGee Banks and Banks (1995) offer a multidimensional approach to integrate the experiences of diverse students into the social studies curriculum. The dimensions include (1) content integration, (2) knowledge construction, (3) prejudice reduction, (4) an equity pedagogy, and (5) an empowering school and social culture. The goal is to integrate the experiences of students while addressing social justice.

Content integration means that the teacher includes the experiences of others beyond the male, white dominated narrative often presented as history. For example, when constructing a unit on World War II, a social studies teacher can create learning opportunities where the students investigate the war from multiple perspectives. In addition to obvious, underrepresented and misrepresented groups like women, teachers can also include specific background perspectives based on the culture of her students. For example, if the class included English language learners from the Dominican Republic, she could incorporate that perspective as well.

Being respectful and inclusive with content integration suggests, "Culturally relevant teachers utilize students' culture as a vehicle for learning" (Ladson-Billings, 2001, p. 161), and culturally responsive teaching frames learning in a multiethnic paradigm promoting agency (Gay, 2010). In addition to developing a multiethnic curriculum, teachers and students also formulate a knowledge foundation of cultural diversity; strive to build a culturally diverse learning community; develop intercultural communication; and implement culturally consistent strategies for learning (Gay, 2002).

The second dimension is knowledge construction, which requires that students critically examine how a dominant perspective shapes the questions and presentations. Textbooks present manifest destiny, for example, as a Western movement. To the Mexicans, it is North, and to certain native tribes, it is East.

Textbooks and other curricular materials almost always present manifest destiny from the Anglo-American perspective and the conquest of savage lands.

The third dimension of equity pedagogy requires that teachers differentiate their strategies based on ethnic and cultural considerations. One fruitful area of research concludes that Mexican-American students learn more effectively when they receive personalized attention from the teacher. Also, according to Banks and McGee Banks, in some situations, Black Americans learn more effectively in cooperative learning groupings. The suggestion is for teachers to utilize many different styles to reach as many types of students as possible.

The fourth dimension is prejudice reduction. From the curricular resources to student conduct, a teacher can actively monitor, model, practice, and implement a safe environment for all students. For example, a teacher can create a brief exercise analyzing the photographs in the textbook and pose the question of whether the images represent them and American society.

The fifth and last dimension is empowerment in the classroom and across the school campus. Beginning with the leadership of the principal, multicultural education requires that educators inspect all aspects of the school. With a goal of empowering minority students, administrators and teachers embark on an agenda to better prepare them.

They also provide underserved students enhanced access to advanced classes while questioning whether traditional procedures such as voting school-wide for homecoming representatives or cheerleaders reinforce dominant culture exclusivity and stereotypes. All the dimensions rest on the foundation that in their vision, teachers value and leverage students' diverse experiences to promote intelligent behavior and social justice.

EXPERIENCE AND JUDGMENT

In experience, concepts and theories become useful instruments in the service of intelligent inquiry and taking action in the world. The instrumentalist does not believe in fixed absolutes and truths, so concepts and theories are never a true representation of reality. The measure of their usefulness is not whether they are true or false, but rather how effective they are in predicting and explaining phenomena. Therefore, the truth of an idea is a *judgment* about how well an idea solves a problem or transforms an indeterminate situation into a determinate one.

Two judgments important for the social studies are moral and historical types. Because *an* experience implies qualitative aspects such as place, time, and other characteristics, it necessarily involves valuations. Valuing takes place in primary experience with the immediate liking or disliking of something had; and in secondary experience as reflections about patterns of conduct related to things like integrity, freedom, rugged individualism, and any other valued behavior (Dewey, 1939). Moreover, conflicting values among individuals and groups supply social and political problems, which are also the materials for the social studies curriculum.

Moral Development as Judgment

At the most fundamental ontological level of analysis, a living creature transacts with the environment to survive. A universal example is the act of breathing, exchanging oxygen for carbon dioxide with the net production of energy to sustain life. The process is physical and involves the expanding and contracting of muscles, the functioning of the bronchioles and alveoli in the lungs, and consequently changes both the person and the surrounding environment. The transaction is *qualitative* because it involves "temporality, spatial location, efficiency, smoothness, and so on, including *value*" (Pamental, 2010, p. 20). The qualities surface in the process and sequence of the breathing event.

In normal circumstances, a person does not concentrate on breathing until something deviates from the norm such as when a boy suffers an allergic reaction or encounters smoke. The situation embodies coughing, and all the events leading to the coughing. For example, maybe as he walked to school, a city bus passed belching diesel fumes. The boy inhaled the noxious pollutants, and then coughed for several seconds while reaching for his asthma inhaler. The qualities of nature provided the boy's experiences as he interacted with the environment in a situation. The boy, in effect, analyzed himself and his surrounding environment to ensure his survival.

The quality of the boy's transaction also had *value* meaning he probably disliked, feared, and was repulsed by his interaction with the bus exhaust. Put another way, these were the immediate qualities of his experience. However, these were not judgments of *reflective morality*, which are based on valued patterns of behavior (Dewey, 1939). In the first case, immediate things are only felt and had. In the second, the reflection focuses on the sequences of activities. Pamental (2010) explains the difference with the example of "honesty."

Humans live in a precarious, changing world, and one can make the judgment that honesty is always a good pattern of behavior for succeeding in business or enhancing social relations. However, being consistently and perpetually honest only works if everyone else does the same. Further, contrary to a moral upbringing, it is undesirable to relegate honesty to habit because one would want to maintain awareness to avoid scams and charlatans, or possibly avert offending another individual, or in an extreme example, to shield state secrets.

Further, experience congruent with the natural world suggests that moral values are not fixed, such as rendering a judgment that something is *always* right or wrong. In effect, making a final judgment of right or wrong implies that previous experiences are *ends*, resulting in a philosophical dead end. Rather, every new situation demands that one draws on prior experiences, connoting "values—those activities, behaviors, qualities of transactions that have been prized in the past—as instruments of reflective inquiry, instead of determinants of 'right' behavior" (p. 21). Reflective inquiry requires that one assess the experience under consideration anew.

Therefore, in experience, value conflicts are synonymous with indeterminate situations, which by nature humans attempt to make determinate with inquiry. Or stated another way, indeterminate situations which humans strive to make determinate, can lead to value conflicts as people can attach different values to the qualities of a situation.

When an individual has *an* experience, the resolution of an indeterminate situation into a determinate one necessitates an active moral judgment, which includes values and things deemed important. The judgment itself constitutes another experience encompassing both objective and subjective elements. Because the problems are real, there are objective elements in the environment that limit solutions or constrain action like the boy's choice to reach for his asthma inhaler rather than waving a magic wand.

How the boy feels and all the immediate qualities comprise the subjective, personal elements, which either reinforce or reject the objective ones. It also potentially leads to the development of habits or sparks doubt about the solution. In other words, the moral development of character always involves objective environmental elements and the subjective evaluation of them.

Historical Judgment

The other type of judgment in experience holding great importance for the social studies is historical. The solving of a problem within a situation entails a process, which inherently indicates a spatial-temporal element of time and place. A simple, mundane example is: A girl is watching television in bed and she becomes thirsty. To solve the problem, she pushes back the covers, leaps out of bed, and walks to the kitchen to slake her thirst. The situation is an existential proposition because the slaking of the thirst is concrete where some change occurs "*from* something *to* something" (*LTI*, p. 221).

When the situation has boundaries of starting and ending, as well as a temporal focus, one labels it an *event*. Defining a historical event involves a judgment. For example, one can ascribe a time from roughly 1939–1946 as World War II, but another person points to the aftermath of World War I as the starting point of the event. Further, all propositions primarily concerning time and the use of judgment to define an event comes from three broad sources: (1) an individual's personal experience; (2) unique events not part of one's personal past; and (3) the judgments of historians.

What all three sources have in common is an individual initiates the process in some present, immediate circumstances. Therefore, one of the delimiting factors is the immediate moment no matter the situation—whether a person is thinking about what happened at breakfast yesterday, a police officer investigating a crime, or a historian making a judgment about who assassinated President Kennedy.

Although in the first case, one may be drawing on personal recollections, the recollections themselves are subjected to judgments about a sequence of events as one interrogates the evidence. A person thinks about yesterday when she first walked her dog, and then after enjoyed a bagel before heading off to work. It is with a high degree of *probability*, rather than complete *certainty*, she can say she ate a bagel within the sequence.

What if she contemplates on the same day whether she ate breakfast? She may run through the same sequence, but perhaps she doubts her recollection. Perhaps it was yesterday that she ate the bagel after walking her dog? In that case, she may consider that, although she does not sense hunger at that moment, she conjectures that soon she will feel hunger pangs. That is to say, the girl's historical judgment in the present encapsulates the past and looks to the future.

In the second case when judgments are made outside of personal recollections, the main difference to the first case is that a person analyzes evidence and then makes inferences about what happened. The police officer uses all available forensic tools and analyses to determine who committed the crime and how. She examines the unique evidence of the case and compares the evidence with past recollections of similar experiences.

The judgments of historians are a subset of the second case because they are judgments outside of personal recollections, but are more restricted in subject matter. Because they involve existential propositions chroniclers make in the present about some specified sequence of events in the past, they usually suffer from a lack of complete, unified evidence and increased complexity relative to the other two cases. In general, the further the historian looks back in time, the more likely she discovers significant gaps in the historical evidence.

Unlike the police officer who follows a protocol in the processing of evidence, the historian self-selects evidence, and then assigns relative weight to each unit to make inferences and draw specific conclusions. She writes about history through the lens of present culture, which profoundly affects the selection process.

The historian also selects subject matter within an infinite continuum. It is physically impossible to write all history and mentally impossible to address all the historical evidence even within a highly delimited period. To Dewey, history had a "double meaning" because when a historian reconstructs the past she also creates a new history reflecting the problems and attitudes of the present. Like the former two cases of personal recollections and unique events outside of direct personal experiences, the judgments of historians are also forward-reaching because they create future paradigms.

Because all history is to and from something, logically, the problems and purposes of the inquiries determine the limitations. However, the historian works in the present, which is not static, but moving in a future direction. History can only march forward to some pending outcome. In other words, a historian writes history from a present point of view, and the selection and valuing of evidence will inevitably be shaped by her perspective rooted in the present. And perhaps most importantly, she contemplates future consequences in her perspective, which will serve as the source of materials for future historians.

The entire endeavor commences within the context of current social interests, and will also influence further directions. For example, if a historical researcher perceives an interest today with a study about the influence of women of color in the space program, the unearthed evidence and conclusions can trigger more investigative activity about the contributions of women in physics, or some other related field. History is continuous and historical findings and contemporary concerns become the starting points for future investigations.

The double nature also implies that in addition to historians looking back to the past to reinterpret it with successive and new social perspectives, they also discover new tools for examining the present and consequences for the future. For example, if the world is in the throes of a populist surge, historians can look to the last populist uprising in the 1880s and 1890s to create meaning of current conditions, and to consider future ramifications.

HISTORY EDUCATION AS INSTRUMENTAL

Perhaps no aspect of Dewey's philosophy inflamed more passion than his assertion that history is instrumental for socializing young people. Mirroring the aim of the social studies to promote civic competence and active, democratic decision making, Dewey's social agenda suggests that students *use* history to study current problems with the ethical goal of enhancing democracy, which consequently improves social relations leading to further individual growth and adaptation. What his critics fail to acknowledge is the continuous nature of history and how severing the present from the past creates a competing, isolated world, which denies students a valuable reservoir of social experience.

Dewey was concerned with the *process* of history in experience, which inherently means that he focused on an individual's history more than social history, particularly in the context of change. *It is the individual's potential to change the social system that matters, not the system molding the individual to the social norm.*

Many critics attack Dewey's instrumentalism as the source of problems with the teaching of social studies because it overly focuses on current events, non-disciplinary pursuits, values student experiences more than subject matter, or fails to include the teaching of disciplinary knowledge (Egan, 1980, 1983; Finn Jr., 2003; Frazee & Ayers, 2003; Hirsch, 1988; Neill, 1960; Rochester, 2003).

Because a critical attribute of pragmatism is the inexorable human condition of experiencing the world in the present, Dewey emphatically rejected the tenet that historians can truly come to know the past or that students should study history for history's sake alone. One illustrative example of this criticism is:

> When history becomes an agent of socializing it begins to develop a different aim from that which distinguishes history as an academic discipline. The aim of history as a discipline is to come to understand the past in its own terms, in its uniqueness, for its own sake and the sake of the pleasure of such understanding.... In socializing we do not aim to bring children to an understanding of the past for its own sake, but rather we use the past in order to focus on the present.... A successful program of socialization will lead to its products sharing attitudes and values, and images of their nation. (Egan, 1983, pp. 201–02)

In a footnote to this passage, the author further asserts,

> What is needed for my argument here . . . is only the simple distinction between the use of history to discover and understand what really happened (hardly an uncomplicated formulation) and the abuse of history which makes it subservient to present interests and present concerns, which focuses all the past on the present, and which destroys the autonomy of past events. (Egan, 1983, p. 213)

What resonates from criticisms like these is a failure to grasp the continuity of history.

Studying history for history's sake does not make sense in Dewey's system of ideas because the natural world can never break from the past. Everything that *is* originated in the past and when a situation severs the connections between past and present, a fantasy realm results that competes with the present (*DE*). In fact, history educators want students to learn to make arguments regarding historical causation. One would have to put on extreme blinders to not consider how causes of historical events of importance might or might not be operative in the present.

In *Reconstruction in Philosophy* (1920), Dewey further contended that the past is only vital in how it addresses the precarious conditions of living today. Individuals acting intelligently in the world incessantly reconstruct their understanding of experience as they contend with a problematic world. The same is true for philosophy as new political and techno-scientific discoveries influence how people view the past and its problems, and yield insights into the moving present. Instead of trying to understand what was unique or different about the past, the past becomes a resource for the advancing present.

Evolution proves that humans can never escape their past. The past provides information about where people originate, and where their reference point commences every day,

> Our personal desires and beliefs, our resources and tools of action, have a past reference having its own hold and reference. The continuity of history means that there is no starting anew; the "new order" forecast by revolutionaries and feared by timid conservatives is impossible. The "new" is that which has just happened, that which deviates from the old and regular. But the meaning of what is "new" cannot be determined apart from its relations to the old, to the integrated happenings of the past. (Austin, 1965, p. 200)

One of the main reasons students find history courses boring today is precisely because most teachers still teach history for history's sake rather than viewing it as a rich resource for today's experiences (Milo, 2015).

SUMMARY

The terms "experience" and "history" are interchangeable. They represent the minimum unit of analysis because they capture how individuals survive in the world using the accumulated wisdom of humanity. Most experiences are primary—crude brushes with the natural world—but they have the potential to lead to thoughtful understanding in secondary experience. Moreover, teachers should value the experiences students bring to school because they provide the prior knowledge and objects for thinking.

In thinking, people make historical and value judgments. When they fail to test and verify their conclusions in the natural world, they develop rigid, erroneous beliefs, which stunt their growth and stymy social relations and progress. Dewey emphasized education as a force in fighting ignorance. Because humans are continuous with nature, history becomes a resource for addressing immediate problems in the quest for adaptation and more growth in experience. And because experience embodies natural qualities, chapter 4 explores the values that supply social problems and nurture student interest.

Chapter 4

Morality

Focus Questions:

1 What are the conditions necessary for students to develop interests?
2 What are the implications of Dewey's valuation theory for the social studies?
3 What lessons should social studies teachers learn from Dewey about character and character education?

The last chapter ended with an example of a social studies learning situation where students used curriculum in their experience to arrive at a settled belief about slavery. The activity began with the teacher exploring student interests and the idea of "method, [which] is concerned with providing conditions so adapted to individual needs and powers to make for the permanent improvement of observation, suggestion, and interpretation" (*HWT*, p. 46).

Building on the illustration, one of the neglected areas of Dewey's education philosophy focuses on the proper role of interest and effort and its instrumental character in guiding an activity to completion (Jonas, 2011). When an individual encounters a problem, habit no longer suffices because the old way of doing something neither fits her needs nor the new situation's circumstances. In order to resolve the issue, she engages in reflective moral activities, which are value judgments. The judgments, in turn, lead to conduct changes, which in the widest sense include all the physical and psychical interactions together with human feelings and emotions.

Acting ethically, moreover, means she also adopts *the habits of reflection* to purposively evaluate and improve her value judgments instrumentally. In other words, she reconstructs her moral practices in response to changing needs and conditions. In addition, to affect something instrumentally is an if-then proposition where she tests value judgments to discover whether the consequences solve the problem or are acceptable in the real world.

And because humans are social beings, she does not consider the effects in isolation, but rather also how the consequences of her judgments influence other individuals. The seeds for conduct manifest in human impulses—the automatic reflexes, instincts, drives, and appetites—naturally endowed in humans to incite movement in the world. Impulses, in turn, are an essential source for interests within a purposive activity.

The development of *interest* can best be understood as a process of discovery as a person's natural impulses help her identify with a course of activity and its successful completion using *effort*. At the same time, effort is guided by *desire*, which keeps an eye on the end-in-view while propelling the activity toward a successful completion given whatever the circumstances are in the immediate moment. Problem solving through an activity, in this manner, is a reflective enterprise.

Dewey contended that the vast social changes over the last several centuries and the complexities of the modern world requires that individuals operate at this level of moral reflective conduct, instead of the unreflective, knee-jerk style of the traditional world of fixed ends and supreme authority. For instance, the medieval world of the Russian serf in the ninth century living in sparsely populated communities within the norms of a morality based on unquestioning subservience and obedience adhered to a fixed hierarchy in exchange for a simple life of stability and certainty.

In contrast, the emergence of contemporary society in all its splendor, hardships, and complex interactions brought people closer together in living arrangements and work. The Industrial Revolution wrought massive social changes and new conflicts. The problems of today require that citizens employ, test, and develop the habits of value judgments, meaning they conduct themselves intelligently as reflective social beings. The main purpose of schools is to change young people from unreflective, impulsive creatures to intelligent moral reflective operators.

In *Theory of the Moral Life* (1932), Dewey claimed that an ethical life was comprised of two types of conduct: the inner, psychical activities of "thought and feeling, ideals and motives, valuation and choice" (pp. viii–ix) (i.e., the psychological), and the outer connections of conduct to the natural world of social relations (i.e., the biological and social sciences). Ethics requires that one addresses the conflicts resulting from the inner and outer dealings,

> It has to study the inner process as *determined by the outer conditions or as changing these outer conditions*, and the outward behavior or institution as *determined by the inner purpose, or as affecting the inner life*. (*TML*, p. ix)

Today, the transformation of the individual student into an intelligent thinker is the domain of developmental psychology.

The teacher's role is to provide a curriculum that aligns to primitive impulses, and together with the needs and capacities of the students, create situations so students can organically discover and explore their interests as a shared venture. The outer world of social relations supplies the field of social studies with its *raison d'être,* as well as the problems to practice reflective moral judgment, and even more importantly, promote the development of the habit to do so.

A vision for social studies teachers is to recognize that the inner imaginative processes originate in the primitive impulses of human nature. Teachers, therefore, are tasked with helping students to identify and harness those impulses into interest and effort. At the same time, to develop moral character means, first, teachers must reflect on the interaction of their own character traits and attitudes and the wider consequences to change their conduct. And second, they must also design learning activities for students to engage periodically in reflective morality.

INTEREST AND EFFORT

As you may recall from the previous chapter, Dewey identified four phases of experience, which one can further subdivide into the noninstrumental primary experiences and instrumental secondary ones (see figure 3.1). This section addresses *the activities* in experience and how human beings operate at three levels of behavior: impulse, habit, and moral reflection. The story begins with birth and the activities of newborns, who mainly follow noninstrumental impulses.

Impulse Psychology

Natural impulses drive a newborn's first interactions with the world. The "discharge" of impulses is an expressive activity, and as Dewey wrote, "Impulse is always differentiated along some more or less specific channel" (*IEE*, 1913, p. 18). Some of the impulse expressions involve an activity toward an external object such as using eyes to follow adult faces, reaching for a rattle, or burping after a meal.

Other activities may not be directed at a particular object, and may include crying, the kicking of feet, or yawning. Even when an activity produces a consequence, such as when the newborn cries from hunger, and a bottle appears to satisfy the need, the young baby has no idea that the crying leads to the need's fulfillment. The baby is merely acting impulsively.

Dewey's read of human nature as constant motion is a form of impulse psychology. Unlike the traditional desire-based schemas, Dewey's novel version begins with activity as the default human state-of-being and the source of impulses, which drive our most basic, instinctual appetites. Dewey points to the activities of children who are in constant activity without any end-in-view, which is also the definition of play (*HWT*, 1910).

Moreover, a psychology based on primitive impulses also suggests that the sources of impulses are flexible and fluid offering opportunities to direct and shape those impulses toward some *desired goal*. When conceived in this manner, impulses are the building blocks for educative experiences and intelligent activity while desires are the fixed goals relative to some end-in-view.

As the newborn matures, repeated experiences reveal consequences in the impulsive activities. In the beginning, the baby undergoes a bowel movement, experiences the resulting discomfort of a soiled diaper, and cries. She cries because of the discomfort, not because she is purposely signaling the need for a fresh diaper. As her experience deepens and widens over time however, she begins to associate the activity of crying with the consequence of a diaper change. The perceiving of consequences—ends-in-views—is the formation of a desire. Consequently, the surrounding environment's reaction to the impulsive activity shapes the desire.

When parents unremittingly respond to the crying, the child develops into a spoiled brat who places her own interests before the consideration of others. Adults that respond discriminately to specific conditions, shape the interests of the child to desired ends, which take into consideration the needs and interests of other claimants. Impulses are malleable and demand expression. When they are organized within an activity, they result in an interest (Anderson, 2014).

To illuminate the point, Dewey turned to the etymology of "*inter-esse*, 'to be between,' points in the same direction" (*IEE*, 1913, p. 18). Interests begin in impulses, undeveloped biological drives that only humans can bring into conscious view. When a person expresses the objects of her interests, they also reveal her underlying impulses, even if they remain embryonic and undeveloped.

Interest and Growth in Education

Any complete experience, meaning the following of an activity to completion, involves some level of interest. However, a learner only develops *genuine interest* through the material presented relative to some activity, which psychologists today call intrinsic motivation (Deci & Ryan, 1985).

When an outside agent like a teacher threatens, cajoles, or bribes a student to complete an activity, the student then reacts by substituting the desirable, genuine interest developed within her psychical being (e.g., completing an essay about the role of women in wartime because of an interest in gender equity) for an undesirable, impure interest (e.g., threat of not passing the course), which at best, results in compliance.

The impure interest is driven by impure effort because like genuine interest, *legitimate effort* only develops as part of a moving activity. In effect, when the learner experiences dissonance (i.e., a problematic situation) she applies effort to initiate the thinking process. The development of interest and the application of effort also require the use of judgment. Together—interest, effort, and judgment—lead to an expanding experience and more growth.

In *Interest and Effort in Education* (1913), Dewey defined interest as the inner state that results when an individual identifies the interaction between a specific object (e.g., concept, or fact, or expression, or idea, etc.) "with the growing self" (p. 7). When the individual perceives the need as so great for self-fulfillment, the person demands it to become whole. Therefore, one grows by identifying with the interaction of the object and one's natural inclinations.

Maslow's Hierarchy

An illustration of this fulfillment is found in Maslow's hierarchy of needs, which preservice teachers usually encounter in a psychology course. Maslow integrated many elements of Dewey's functional psychology into his theory of motivation where the interaction of the psychical and outward behavior results in an active adaptation. Often represented in a pyramid graphic, the most basic needs, physiological and safety, support the higher ones, love/belonging, esteem, and ultimately, self-actualization.

The highest need, self-actualization, mirrors Dewey's conception of interest in the service of self-expressive activity:

> Even if all these needs are satisfied, we may still often (if not always) expect that a new discontent and restlessness will soon develop, unless the individual is doing what *he* or *she*, individually, is fitted for. Musicians must make music, artists must paint, poets must write if they are to be ultimately at peace with themselves. What humans *can* be, they *must* be. They must be true to their own nature. This need we may call self-actualization. (Maslow, 1987, p. 22)

Further, Maslow credited Dewey for combining impulse with cognition in defining a need and explaining the possibility of a person fulfilling a need with gratification (i.e., attaining pleasure) or not.

Developing Student Interests

One of the teacher's main duties is to be an impulse psychologist, who helps her students perceive these inchoate expressions, and working with them in a collaborative curriculum undertaking, develop their impulses as sources of interest in learning. Teachers should ask students questions and listen attentively. They should observe them interacting with others and survey them formally and informally every available chance to gather their likes and dislikes, what they do in their free time, and who they enjoy spending time with. Using these data, the teacher then designs learning activities—preferably offering choices—where the students can explore and realize their interests.

Perhaps a social studies teacher in a global history course discovers that some of her students are interested in hip-hop music. She explores with them the reasons why the appeal is so strong including the genre's identification with Black and Latino culture, personal expression, the valuing of inner-city identity, etc. Working with these students, she can create entry points in the curriculum for them to explore and develop their interests by studying identity in other cultures, or discovering how people express themselves in the urban centers of ancient empires like Rome.

Although the interest in the above example is hip-hop music, the teacher would be misguided in thinking that focusing merely on a genre of music will result in an effective motivational schema. The teacher and students must dig deeper and look at the impulses because these will lead to new interests that students only faintly perceive. Further, the development of interest within an activity produces a welling of pleasure.

Interest and Pleasure

When designing learning situations, especially new teachers should heed Dewey's wisdom to avoid the pleasure trap. As when the baby *feels* discomfort in the earlier example, our crude brushes with the world in primary experience can also produce *immediate* pleasure. In fact, human drive and appetite for pleasure also rounds an experience when it is carried to completion as part of an activity. Dewey distinguished between the type of pleasure from the direct excitation of our senses with the pleasure received when an interest latches onto an object and expands with the object until consummation:

> There are two types of pleasure. One is the accompaniment of activity. It is found wherever there is successful achievement, mastery, getting on. It is the personal phase of an outgoing energy. This sort of pleasure is always absorbed in the activity itself. It has no separate existence. This is the type of pleasure found in legitimate interest. Its source lies in meeting the needs of the organism. The other sort of pleasure arises from contact. It marks receptivity. Its stimuli are external. It exists by itself as a pleasure, not as the pleasure of activity. (*IEE*, 1913, p. 12)

Teachers sometimes confuse the two (Jonas, 2011).

In the classroom, the psychological goal is to have students identify with an object, and then carry through with an activity based on the resultant interest in that object. In this sense, the student derives pleasure from successfully achieving or mastering the object through the activity. The individual's interest is "a form of self-expressive activity" (*IEE*, 1913, p. 21), an act of unfolding, or being in the process of becoming; or put another way, the consummation of the activity creates pleasure because it fulfills a need. One cannot separate the interest developed with the object nor the activity carrying it to full fruition.

Much like when teachers merely focus on overt interests, another misguided practice occurs when teachers address student boredom and disengagement. In some cases, they resort to making instruction pleasurable without regard to interest (Jonas, 2011; Okan, 2003). When a teacher *makes something interesting*, the resulting situation creates a breach between outer and inner energies, a discordant wedge between a pleasurable outer activity and an intrinsically pleasurable inner one.

For example, when the teacher offers a candy reward for completing a worksheet about the Aztecs, she is appealing to an outer pleasure, a separate activity (i.e., eating candy) outside the curriculum. Conversely, when the teacher realizes her students have an interest in how children and adolescents fit into society, she attends to her students' inner energies and provides opportunities for them to *inquire* into the Aztec social system. During inquiry, students may discover that some things are timeless such as parental love, and at the same time, they may uncover the militaristic aspects of the Aztec children's upbringing, which the students may connect to a study of Greek Sparta at some other time. The opportunities for exploring interests are infinite, but can only originate from within.

Teachers cannot make something interesting because the interest can only be called forth or developed within the person toward that object. When teachers employ "the sugar-coating method," not only does it violate the principle of interest, but Dewey also explains that it creates "a subject-matter existing wholly independently of the pupil's own activity" (*IEE*, p. 33). That is to say, making something fun without properly cultivating interest subsumes the learner's process for growth and understanding.

Other types of sweetening include teachers delivering content with flashy social media, young children watching educational programs featuring cartoon characters, or teachers bribing students with free media center passes for completing assignments. One outcome is that children often become overly excited in one instant, and bored in the next, something any social studies teacher can attest to who has ever exceeded the limit of projecting an instructional video beyond the point of interest (*IEE*, 1913).

It follows then, sometimes students become addicted to the pleasure "as the drunkard is upon his dram" (p. 13), rather than perceiving an interest in the interaction with the activity. Seeking pleasure for the sake of a candy reward (or any other type of direct pleasure) creates a separate, disjointed, competing activity to the educative one where primitive effort substitutes for genuine interest.

In short, students become interested in objects, ideas, concepts, and all other elements of the curriculum only when they come to recognize that through the physical and psychical interactions, they will make themselves complete. Dewey labeled the movement forward "desire" (*IEE*, p. 49), and because the movement involves new activities with conflicting values and the accompanying stresses (i.e., the encountering of problems), effort is required. In other words, *students summon interest and effort manifesting in desire to address a perceived problem through thinking.*

Effort, Motivation, and Thinking

Although "bare effort, or strain" (*IEE*, p. 49) can substitute for genuine interest when teachers impose punishments or lavish rewards, truly educative effort can only occur in partnership with genuine interest within the movement of an expanding activity. In fact, they are complementary forces where the impulses underlying interest provide the mental nourishment while effort propels the activity forward and all the while desire keeps an eye on the end-in-view as the activity proceeds through successive stages.

Encountering obstacles forces a learner to bring the ends of an activity into her consciousness. It moves her from a state of impulse or habit into one of active thinking. Effective teachers appeal to a student's prior experiences, abilities, and interests, while integrating new curriculum for the student to intelligently carry out an activity with a new ending. The more mature and developed the learner, the more remote and indirect is the ending. Only interest and effort can carry a multifactor activity to a long completion. Indeed, "'Motive' is the name for the end or aim in respect to its hold on *action*, its power to *move*" (*IEE*, 1913, p. 60).

What happens when the habits of past experiences fail a person in some present predicament? Because the emotions attached to effort embody conflicting predilections related to the desire to go on and the hardship generated by obstacles encountered along the way, the situation produces "*mental* stress: a peculiar emotional condition of combined desire and aversion" (*IEE*, p. 49).

Stress, in turn, signals to the person that it is time to think. Whether one decides to put forth effort and for how long depends upon the exercise of judgment. Perhaps the individual considers: Do I have the will or purpose to follow through? Is the end attainable? Or do the means justify the ends? The learner monitors herself throughout the successive stages adapting to changing conditions, switching means relative to the ends, or perhaps dropping the activity altogether judging the ends to be less important given the amount of energy required for successful completion:

> The true function of the conditions that call forth effort is, then, first, to make an individual more *conscious of the end and purpose of his actions*; secondly, to *turn his energy from blind, or thoughtless, struggle into reflective judgment.* (*IEE*, 1913, p. 53)

In experience terms, a problematic or indeterminate situation is the catalyst for the individual to transition from non-cognitive primary to inferential secondary experience. The exercise of reflective judgment in secondary experience means the person is using *desire* to monitor the end-in-view and to either make adjustments or to scrap the entire endeavor. These decisions involve *valuation*.

VALUATION AND ETHICS

One may recollect from the discussion in the last chapter on experience that because we live in a qualitative world (i.e., made of tangible qualities) people like and dislike objects as part of an experience or activity. One may also recall from chapter 1 how Dewey developed instrumentalism as an antidote to classical philosophy's emphasis on the stable aspects of existence as represented in the Greek word *physis*:

> For centuries, until, say, the sixteenth and seventeenth centuries, nature was supposed to be what it is because of the presence within it of ends. In their very capacity as ends they represented complete or perfect Being. All natural changes were believed to be striving to actualize these ends as the goals toward which they moved by their own nature. (*TV*, 1939, p. 2)

Instead, in his naturalism Dewey conceived a philosophy consistent with evolution and based on interaction and possibility, roughly akin to *techne*. He rejected the classical idea of fixed ends in intrinsic and extrinsic value, and instead, embraced a scientific approach.

This section begins with a discussion about the importance of valuation in human nature. When the act of valuing leads to value judgments the student is engaging in reflective behavior, which propagates a virtuous cycle where she perceives new interests and desires. Likewise, she can instrumentally test the value judgments on real problems. The experimental testing is a means-to-consequences relationship, which subsequently follows that the context of the situation is an independent variable. This experimental approach also illustrates the rejection of classical philosophy's fixed and final ends.

Valuation Theory

Valuation theory is concerned with why, how, and to what extent a person values something. On the "affective-motor" (*VT*, p. 13) level, one can like or dislike something as *prizing* or *caring for* as a first-order, primitive valuing without making it an object of second-order reflection. On a second-order level, one can *appraise* something in an instrumental way by deliberating how effectively the object of inquiry leads to the desired consequences.

Primitive Valuations

At the primary level of experiencing the world, crude interactions produce valuations that tend to either move *positively toward* objects such as when a baby's eyes lock on a parent; or they move *negatively away* from objects as when a diner sneezes after eating something with too much pepper. Also in immediate circumstances, the valuing of *using* objects with little or no cognition can occur as when one habitually reaches for a salt shaker to season her food (see figure 3.1).

A person can also express a valuation primitively or as ejaculatory. A person riding a horse may say, "Whoa!" or a child touching a pointed object may scream, "Ouch!" or a student grabbing a laptop computer from a cart may interject, "Score!" However, these are not value judgments because an individual must first initiate an evaluation or appraisal of the situation. The latter example can become a second-order value judgment if the student brings to consciousness whether she ought to use the laptop to complete the required assignment (the valuing). Then, the answer is the value judgment.

Valuings, Desires, and Interests

Social studies educators should always strive to encourage their students to exercise value judgments. Implicitly, students would spend more of their time in reflective activity solving practical problems dear to them and necessary for the preservation of democratic society. Moreover, value judgments lead to new valuings, which have two major implications for learning.

First, the new valuings transform into additional and novel interests and desires. In other words, the process of appraising or valuing, leading to a value judgment, expands the student's world to seek new means and ends-in-views. What if the teacher orders the laptop cart because she wants the students to investigate theories about how the ancient Egyptians constructed pyramids? Perhaps the teacher selects websites featuring contradictory theories, and subsequently, some of the students become confused.

The mental stress of how to proceed provokes one student to ask herself some questions: Should I give up? Should I raise my hand and ask the teacher for help? Should I ask the student next to me for assistance? Using imagination, she psychically works out the means and contemplates the consequences of each of her choices. She rules out giving up because she is concerned with falling behind the other students and she also concludes, if she does give up, her grade will drop significantly.

Next, she looks around the classroom and determines that the teacher is busy helping others and will not be available for some time. She then decides that her best course of action is to ask the boy sitting next to her. He suggests that she read about the pyramids in Wikipedia first, and then visit the other websites because that is how he made sense of the competing theories.

In this case, all the perceived consequences themselves become objects of valuation, and they alter her ends-in-view, leading to a new valuing. Moreover, this valuing or appraising of consequences is practical because it results in a new course of action. And because a course of action is another term for desire, it also reflects a change in desires and the connected interests.

Second, one can evaluate the instrumental nature of value judgments because the new valuings and appraisals are used to solve real problems. The student can assess how well the consequence worked for her. She follows her classmate's strategy and reads an overview of the different theories in Wikipedia, and then reads the details of the various theories from the other websites. She concludes that the new valuing (i.e., appraising the consequences of reading about the theories in Wikipedia first) solves her conundrum.

The student does much more than value objects (i.e., if-then propositions) as part of learning about the ancient Egyptian pyramids; she also adds to her repertoire of how to engage in more intelligent valuings, leading to additional appraisals. In effect, she is coordinating desires (i.e., ends-in-view), and using appraisals to modify and adapt them, which systematically result in interests.

Means-End Relationships

Another significant contribution Dewey made to philosophy was to reject the classical notion that something could have intrinsic or extrinsic value. An example is: water is good, which is an a priori deduction based on the idea that water as good is a fixed end. Instead, he claimed that value could only be part of a purposive activity.

For instance, drinking water is good when one is thirsty or swimming in water to exhaustion and drowning is always bad. Moreover, when an individual uses desire to monitor an end-in-view, she is engaging in an ethical or moral valuation as she balances competing means, considers rejecting the ends-in-view, or adopts another tact to meet her objectives.

The problem, according to Dewey, was that moral theory was still stuck in the classical world. Despite the vast material progress made with advancement in the technosciences (i.e., the application of technology with the scientific method), human relations remained mired in the old way of thinking. The scientific method discovers the propositions and laws of the natural world without fixed ends.

Contextualism

The context, conditions, environment, backdrop, experience, situation, or any other term designating the operative background within a unit of time supports the foundations of modern science. The Scientific Revolution was a rejection of conceiving the world as constituted by fixed ends in favor of an experimental approach to the natural world. For example, Copernicus' heliocentric model was based on observation and empirical evidence. It eventually supplanted the fixed, geocentric model originally conceived by the ancient Greeks that held moral and cultural sway throughout the Middle Ages.

The same proves true for all modern scientific principles. Even the most sophisticated concepts applying to quantum mechanics like Heisenberg's uncertainty principle show the mere act of measuring one property limits the ability to measure other properties accurately (*EN*). Any natural interaction requires a context. Like the marvels of science and engineering, one of Dewey's contributions is recognizing that social relations and human conduct can also progress if society's members consciously reject fixed ends.

A priori fixed ends have always regulated much of human conduct. Traditional moral theory and ethical living required unquestioning obedience to certain precepts of what was good and right. Quite often throughout history, ruling classes formulated rigid principles to maintain their grasp on power and sometimes oppress others to maintain control and secure material comfort. Throughout history leading theorists have argued that democratic societies were unstable. In effect, adhering to traditional morals and ethics can hold back both individuals and societies from advancing to their potentials.

When people do not have opportunities to experiment with means and the resultant ends, their growth is obstructed and others deny them the opportunity to discover better ways of living. An extreme example is the Jim Crow laws that surfaced across the South in the post–Civil War Reconstruction period.

Restricting people of color from participating socially, economically, and politically certainly harmed many individuals in their abilities to solve problems affecting their growth. Likewise, it also harmed society in lost economic and cultural production, and undermined democracy by furthering the belief that classes of people were unfit to share in democratic governance.

MORAL PHILOSOPHY

At some point in the mid-twentieth century, Dewey's connection to the social studies began to dissolve into the background. Perhaps because Dewey fell out of popular favor during many periods both during his life and posthumously, or maybe because he established the foundations of his philosophy so long ago that other people's ideas overshadowed his precedents, but the reality is that with the dawn of the turbulent 1960s, educators looked less to Dewey to ground their reform efforts.

Social studies scholars, for example, pointed to Shirley Engle's seminal article in a 1960 edition of *Social Education* as the intellectual underpinnings leading to the New Social Studies Movement of the 1960s where he argued for a social studies approach to learning:

> My theme is a very simple one. It is that, in teaching the social studies, we should emphasize decision making as against mere remembering. We should emphasize decision making at two levels: at the level of deciding what a group of descriptive data means, how these data may be summarized or generalized, what principles they suggest; and also decision making at the level of policy determination, which requires a synthesis of facts, principles, and values usually not all found on one side of any question. (Engle, 1960, p. 301)

Clearly, this call for a decision-making approach was steeped in Dewey's system of ideas. Further, a survey of the literature in the 1960s and after reveals that authors infrequently attribute original, Deweyan ideas to Dewey. They are more likely to acknowledge Paolo Freire's critical stance or Jerome Bruner's constructivist philosophy, although the ideas trace back to Dewey (e.g., Massialas, 1992).

Further, in the 1970s the emphasis shifted away from the New Social Studies program and toward an interest in moral education (Fraenkel, 1981; Lieberman, 1975; Merelman, 1979; Stahl, 1979). Although Dewey's instrumentalism (and the work of the pragmatists in general) supplied the intellectual foundation for moral education, once again, many in the field ignored Dewey's profound contributions. Likewise, Dewey's moral education theory was context-dependent and value-inclusive.

When Lawrence Kohlberg developed a theory of moral development in the 1970s, he overshadowed Dewey's reflective morality. Kohlberg believed that an innate, transcendental justice value emerged within individuals in reaction to social contexts. Dewey, on the other hand, did not limit his theory to one main value. This section traces the sources of traditional moral judgment, describes Dewey's radical repositioning of the field, and then looks to the social studies for character education.

Dewey's Moral Life

In Dewey's most comprehensive work on moral theory, *Theory of the Moral Life* (1932), he identified three categories of traditional moral theory as teleological, jural, and virtue theories. Teleological theories attempt to ascertain a supreme fixed end, and to act virtuous or right is to act in accordance with Good. Jural, also called deontological theory, seeks to discover supreme principles and moral laws where a person acts in accordance with Rules (e.g., Kohlberg's theory). Virtue theories, on the contrary, rely on approbation and disapprobation, as well as acclaim and criticism, to enforce customary morality.

The problem for Dewey was that none of the fixed end traditional moral theories sufficiently serve a world of perpetual and accelerating change with myriad conflicting values. At the same time, Dewey did not completely reject custom, and instead suggested that traditional codes of conduct and legal proclamations can serve as data points for reflective activity, again reflecting his philosophy as a middle position.

Additionally, Dewey turned to the emerging fields of biological and social sciences to provide insights into human conduct. And lastly, he proposed that the collective insights of Eastern and Western intellectuals over the centuries provide another rational basis for moral theory.

Much like science achieved beginning in the sixteenth century, moral judgment in contemporary life demands a similar reconstruction based on scientific principles, contextualism, and an unrepentant focus on the individual. Moreover, like his value judgment theory, Dewey conceived earlier societies functioning based on custom and unreflective impulses, which can never provide the conditions nor generate the problems for addressing contemporary moral dilemmas. Rather, he argued that modern times require a new reflective morality.

Habits

Habits develop in human beings as socially shaped modes of behavior within a particular activity or they are customary ways of responding to environing conditions, suggesting, "they are active means, means that project themselves, energetic and dominating ways of acting" (Dewey, 1922, p. 25). The problem with habits and moral theory is twofold: First, much of what is habitual in terms of morality surfaced at an earlier time, and was passed down through successive generations, or as Dewey stated, "An individual usually acquires the morality as he inherits the speech of his social group" (p. 58). And second, because habits are unreflective behaviors, they are not subject to an individual's reflective attention.

Habits are essential for intelligent behavior because humans cannot function efficiently in the modern era if they must problem-solve to overcome every obstacle they repeatedly encounter. At the same time, habits emerging from long-ago customs and impressed on young minds resulting in nonreflective, direct valuations most often leads to dogmatism, indoctrination, and "inveterate prejudice" (*TML*, p. 126).

The problem is that the original circumstances under which the habits first developed have long receded into the past, making them irrelevant or worse, dangerous, in today's world. In fact, Dewey warned us, "It is almost impossible for later reflection to get at and correct that which has become unconsciously part of the self. The warped and disturbed will seem natural" (p. 126). This is another reason why Dewey believed so strongly in progressive education as a corrective counterbalance to habitual morality and the formation of a reflective citizenry.

He placed his focus on young people before their impulses hardened into entrenched, sclerotic habits. Instead, he advocated an education for the development of flexible habits, always questioning the methods and outcomes, as well as the inquiry tools themselves using hypotheses, observations, experimentation, critical thinking, and prognostication. He was not against the older generation teaching the younger generation habits if the habits were grounded in intelligence. In other words, the origins of habits should only come from intelligent conduct.

A Moral Self

What can Dewey teach us about a moral self? His version of a reflective morality encompasses all the elements of a modern society based on diversity, pluralism, inclusivity, receptivity, value conflicts, democracy, and a focus on a changing environment. He concluded,

> The self should be *wise* or prudent, looking to an inclusive satisfaction and hence subordinating the satisfaction of an immediately urgent single appetite; it should be *faithful* in acknowledgment of the claims involved in its relations with others; it should be solicitous, *thoughtful*, in the award of praise and blame, use of approbation and disapprobation, and finally, should be *conscientious* and have the active will to discover new values and to revise former actions. (*TML*, p. 147)

The admonition for teachers is to also heed his advice and appraise the consequences of what they do because social contexts change, and they must also change if they wish to promote moral growth in their students.

Teacher Character Traits and Attitudes

A major theme advanced throughout this book has been about how teachers' entrenched attitudes about custom, citizenship, curriculum, and related matters lead them to a citizenship transmission or social science approach to teaching, which potentially results in a lopsided emphasis on the fixed aspects of content and information at the expense of a curriculum that transcends dualism by addressing social issues with the appropriate disciplinary concepts. Dewey offers a way forward in his instrumental theory of value judgments and character.

When humans combine their impulses with thinking, *character* emerges as the force of will resulting in a consistent conduct. The moral self is constituted of character traits, which drive an individual into certain channels in pursuit of ends. The individual can then evaluate the effectiveness of a given character trait in achieving the desired ends. In the same regard, one's conduct has a habitual quality predisposed to either reinforce those same character traits, or the conduct combines with the character trait and moves along the same impulse.

Dewey asserted that the immediate valuing of attitudes such as those tied to character must be subjected to second-order appraising; meaning teachers *subsequently* evaluate the wider consequences of their own conduct. These appraisals have the potential to confirm prized attitudes or move teachers to seek means to change the undesirable ones. *And here lies one of the greatest lessons: teachers should always contextually evaluate their attitudes, and then allow themselves the flexibility and willingness to deliberate consequences.*

If the interaction between a teacher's conduct and instructional strategies results in consequences where students score poorly on high-quality assessments, appear disinterested, exhibit confusion, engage in continuous disruption, or any other negative outcomes, the teacher should resist placing the blame on students, and begin with critically appraising her own attitudes and values in efforts to influence her own character traits into acceptance of a moral reflective stance. In this manner, she can transform her conduct.

Clearly, the dominant citizenship transmission/social science approach does not work in an increasingly pluralistic and diverse society because instrumentally it is exclusive rather than inclusive (Barr et al., 1978). In the same way, promoting critically reflective behavior in student character is a proper role of the social studies.

Character Education

Dewey's reflective morality mirrors his account of thinking and value judgments in experience and the means-ends relationship. In the normal sense of the word "appraisal" refers to the end or consequence of a specified conduct. However, Dewey presents an account where the agent—while appraising—is constantly adjusting the means to either reach the original end-in-view or a new end-in-view, which is informed by the changing means.

By focusing on the wider consequences, the goal is for individuals to use reflective appraisal to direct future conduct with an eye for solving problems.

A person's impulses and habits supply the initial data with immediate valuings. When she tests the data in experience, she appraises or evaluates the consequences after acting on them. The data come from three sources: one's desires, the claims of other people, and the approval or disapproval others make of her conduct. These data points are not transcendent and the individual uses them as hypotheses to realize and shape consequences.

The social studies, founded in the early twentieth century and coming of age during the Great Depression, provides a controversial curriculum for character education. Dewey envisioned that students would come together with others different from themselves and critically analyze traditional institutions and mores with a goal of developing and embracing a new set of mutual mores to resolve disputes and guide associated living. Within this system of ideas, the *warrant* of existing conditions requires that one develop moral views taking account the people from all social groups and strata. Even how one takes account is subject to critical analysis and change.

A Social Studies Reflective Moral Inquiry Model

Aside from his brief experience at the Laboratory School, Dewey spent much of his adult life logically working through a philosophical system embedded with numerous theories related to education, but left it up to others to devise specific and prescriptive activities.

The question social studies educators should be asking themselves is: What are the characteristics of a meaningful moral reflective activity today? The elements should include:

- Using the social studies curriculum to investigate, analyze, and deliberate moral dilemmas;
- Respecting individual, diverse, and plural perspectives in a participatory social activity;
- Resisting manipulation and indoctrination, especially directed from the teacher;
- Avoiding moral relativism (i.e., something is true or false relative to an established position);
- Evaluating the consequences of the student-derived positions; and
- Recognizing and valuing diverse perspectives through a shared collaborative effort for identifying common moral principles (Lieberman, 1975; Mason, 2016; Merelman, 1979; Pamental, 2010; Selznick, 1992; Simon, 2002).

Guidry (2008) developed a reflective moral inquiry framework for the social studies involving six student steps: (1) Introduction of the problem; (2) Hypothesis formation; (3) Exploration and evaluation of the evidence; (4) Translation and interpretation of the evidence; (5) Evaluation of the hypothesis; and (6) Formation of principle. To do so the teacher must scaffold and facilitate instruction with resources and questions.

The first step is for the teacher to introduce the students to a problem that connects to their experiences and the social studies curriculum such as a scenario containing a moral dilemma about whether a president should use a nuclear strike to repel a rogue nation. The discussion works best with the entire class allowing the maximum wealth of ideas to surface.

In the second step, hypothesis formation, the teacher places students in small, heterogeneous groupings. The students collectively develop a hypothesis, which leads to a plan to address the problem. The teacher circulates among groups encouraging the students to review and revise their hypotheses as they respectfully evaluate the diverse perspectives within the groups.

With the exploration and evaluation of evidence in the third step, the students begin the journey of evaluating their hypotheses using historical and contemporary resources. Depending on the age and skill-level of the students, the teacher can collaborate with them to identify and select the resources they will use to either confirm or refute their hypotheses. The students will also be able to practice the lifelong skill of weighing biases in the sources and materials (Banks & Banks, 2010).

In step four, translation and interpretation of evidence, students identify patterns in the evidence that relate to their hypotheses. This means they develop criteria for judgment. The teacher provides guiding questions in advance to facilitate the process. The students utilize the criteria, consequently, in step five to evaluate the relationship between their hypotheses and the evidence. Once again, the students are encouraged to review and revise the hypotheses.

In the last and sixth step, formation of principle, the author suggests a Socratic seminar discussion to assist the entire class in developing an ethical principle. The final principle is to be generalizable and transferable to new situations, accommodate multiple and diverse perspectives, and have universal applications.

Furthermore, every step provides the teacher multiple opportunities to use instructional grouping strategies that promote maximum student participation like cooperative group work. This moral reflective activity represents an exemplar of a Deweyan activity where student interests drive the process to a conclusion as they make sense together with the aid of a skilled teacher!

SUMMARY

Decades of research point to the conclusion that in many if not most instances, social studies teachers implement the curriculum with little focus on helping students develop their interests for a variety of practical reasons, as well as unperturbable beliefs about the nature and purposes of the social studies. Absent interest, many students languish engaging with materials unreflectively and with minimal effort. In these circumstances, teachers may resort to rewards or punishments blaming students or school conditions for the lack of engagement.

Unlike the classical philosophical world of fixed and predetermined outcomes, in Dewey's system of ideas there are only two fixed concepts congruent with nature: change and the means-ends relationship. Humans identified the importance of this relationship hundreds of years ago in science, which unleashed a torrent of experimental progress. Dewey believed the next frontier for progress is for people to use the means-ends relationship to solve social problems. Therefore, social studies teachers should *wholeheartedly* embrace it to examine their own character traits, and just as importantly, they should select content and develop activities that allow students to build their own skills in problem solving and to augment moral reflective thinking appropriate for citizens in a democratic and open society. The reader may be more familiar with this relationship as thinking and inquiry.

Chapter 5

Inquiry

Focus Questions:

1. How does inquiry facilitate knowledge as a production process?
2. Why is "doing the social studies" inquiry?
3. In what ways do the Common Core State Standards reflect Dewey's approach to education?

The heart of the social studies curriculum is inquiry just like the soul of instrumentalism is the live creature's encounter with hesitation, doubt, and indeterminate situations. Dewey's radical, Darwinian reframing of philosophy's most essential starting points around what exists (ontology) and what counts as knowledge (epistemology) places the live creature's encounters with a problematic situation in a central focus. In the quest for survival and growth, organisms adapt in a changing environment, and through natural selection, variations occur because of that adaptation over time.

Humans emerge as the most intelligent beings because only they developed the ability to bring problems to awareness, and through reflective activity, consider and deliberate the means while considering the consequences. The process entails phases of adjustments to both the means and the ends because each informs the other. Moreover, the solving of problems involves conceptual tools or instruments, hence the name "instrumentalism." Once again, the key to understanding Deweyan philosophy for the social studies is how it is instrumental in our interdisciplinary relationships of studying social problems, and reconstructing an individual's experiences.

The chapter begins with a return to Dewey's ontology and a contrasting with classical philosophy. In Dewey's system of ideas, inquiry leads to a production process where theory and practice unite in the phases of *an* experience. When social studies educators refer to "doing" history, geography, or any other focused subject matter, they are placing the object of learning in an inquiry process.

In addition, when inquiry is combined with the promotion of citizenship, teachers must also provide opportunities for students to identify, analyze, and suggest solutions to social problems, including controversial public issues (CPI). The process also requires that teachers implement effective discussion techniques. However, research shows that teachers often avoid CPI and are not skilled in directing discussions, which leads to a bland, teacher-led curriculum.

Next, because students often use technology in social studies inquiry, the subsequent section first recognizes Dewey as an early pioneer in a philosophy of technology, and then suggests some guidelines for integrating digital tools and artifacts. In sum, a tool is an object that can only act on other objects. Tools are never simply conceptual abstractions of human thought, but rather they are always engaged in a context as part of an experience.

And, finally, the chapter ends with a discussion about how the Common Core State Standards (CCSS) movement and subsequent adoption of the NCSS C3 Framework reflect Dewey's inquiry ideal. *A vision for social studies teachers is to enact an inquiry curriculum where students have opportunities to engage with contemporary problems, and then consider possibilities and consequences leading to social action.*

A RETURN TO DEWEY'S ONTOLOGY

As stated many times throughout this work, the reason Dewey wrote so prolifically about education was that he rationalized that society's most significant challenge was to promote the individual's intelligent engagement with the contemporary, complex world. In fact, the complexity of the modern world *demanded* intelligent interactions to create a social world that would maximize human potential and freedom.

In Dewey's theory of nature, "intelligence" displaced classical philosophy's "reason," which served as a fixed end in Greek thought. Classical philosophy suggested that humans were preprogrammed to attain some predetermined outcome where knowledge was possible in the immediacy. Dewey looked to nature and evolution for guidance, and instead of some a priori knowledge that one's mind could come to know, he began with the premise that all natural processes over time reached ends, and humans could only discover knowledge within these processes. In effect, he eliminated philosophy's dualisms, as well as the anthropocentric bias inherent in traditional systems.

When evolution and nature serve as the backdrop for inquiry and epistemology, four consequences result. First, unlike prior philosophical systems, instrumentalism treats inquiry not as a detached evaluation, but instead as a practical exercise to real-life problems. Second, the old metaphysical categories of traditional philosophies only describe the stable aspects of existence, so Dewey constructed a new ontological terminology that captures both stability and change with application to all beings.

Third, within the stable and changing phases of an individual's experience, the construction of knowledge becomes a production process, which can never attain a final, idealized form as certainty or truth. And fourth, these consequences cumulatively support a skill-based inquiry approach to learning, meaning the social studies curriculum becomes instrumental for improving the conditions for associated living and reconstructing the experience of the learner with inquiry.

The Nature of Inquiry

Another of the many reasons that readers often misunderstand Dewey is because he often used different terms to describe the same process. One prominent example of how Dewey used multiple terms applies to "inquiry," which he also called *logic, thinking, technology,* and *continuity of experience* depending on the period and circumstances.

To further complicate matters, Dewey also operationalized inquiry into smaller units and the *stages of inquiry* became another name for *intelligence.* In the late 1920s, he presented the Gifford Lecture Series, which became memorialized in *The Quest for Certainty* (1929) where he explicitly naturalized intelligence after scrutinizing the fixed nature of reason:

> Intelligence on the other hand is associated with judgment; that is, with selection and arrangement of means to effect consequences and with choice of what we take as our ends. A man is intelligent not in virtue of having reason which grasps first and indemonstrable truths about fixed principles, in order to reason deductively from them to the particulars which they govern, but in virtue of his capacity to estimate the possibilities of a situation and to act in accordance with his estimate. In the large sense of the term, intelligence is as practical as reason is theoretical. (Dewey, 1929, p. 213)

Intelligence embodies both the psychical and the outward acting with some means to reach the desired end.

Intelligence begins with a judgment, which is an initiation of the adjustment of means and refinement of ends—a process the reader most likely recognizes as the only "fixed" aspect of Deweyan thought, the means-to-end relationship. In philosophical terms, these represent the stable aspects or "forms." As Boisvert (1988) observed, "Dewey's choice of 'intelligence' as a term to signify this procedure is well considered from an etymological point of view. The term means 'selecting from among'" (p. 120).

The problematic situation provides the "complex whole" (p. 120) for selecting the elements to arrive at the most satisfactory conclusion. In other words, inquiry is the soul of instrumentalism because humans solve their problems by selecting solutions inherent to a uniquely problematic *context* and with a specific *purpose*. This frame of reference captures the "inner experimentation" (*EN*, p. 166) and outward action for resolving the problem.

Dissolving the inner/outer dualism represents a radical departure from classical philosophy because *reason*, viewed as a fixed end, delineates a separation from the inquirer, who becomes the passive receiver of the ideas separated or inadequately aligned with the frame of reference. In some of his most consequential naturalism works—*Experience and Nature* (1929), *Art as Experience* (1934), and *Logic the Theory of Inquiry* (1938)—Dewey cast classical philosophy as the foil to show that evolution and science point to inquiry as being continuous with nature.

The Unification of Theory and Practice in a Problematic Situation

The previous section alleges that inquiry in a problematic situation unifies theory and practice toward a satisfying resolution. But, how does that means-to-ends readjustment and refinement work in inquiry? Hickman (2001) describes the process as a business arrangement:

> In the hands of the productive pragmatist, then, theory and practice become equal partners as phases of inquiry. Working together, they orient themselves not just to the analysis of the past or present, but to plans for the future. Like good business partners, they are always negotiating with one another about the feasibility, design, cost and marketability of potential products. Theory keeps an eye on practice, making sure that options are kept open, that imagination enters into the design stage, and that potential products are coherent with the larger goals of the firm. Practice keeps an eye on theory, making sure that design and production goals are not too ambitious or too fanciful, that products correspond to the needs of the market, that inventories of products and spare parts are maintained, and that the cash flow is sufficient to start the next project. Together, theory and practice engage in a conversation that constantly adjusts means to ends-in-view, and ends-in-view to the means at hand. The goal of the partnership is not merely action, but production. The goal of the partnership is continual adjustment to changing situations by means of the development of enhanced tools and new products. (p. 180)

The settled product of inquiry is knowledge. The production process implies that knowledge is never a finished product and the inquirer must hold it tentatively as she gathers new data in varying conditions.

Knowledge as Production

Several ontological assumptions underlie the knowledge-production process, and Dewey described them in granular detail (*LTI*). All logical forms (i.e., means-to-consequence activities) originate in doubt (i.e., the organism encountering problems) and manifest in a quest to control inquiry to arrive at a settled state of *knowledge* and *belief*. And because the knowledge-belief outcome is unique to the circumstances of a peculiar problem in the real world with a time and place, Dewey employed the term "warranted assertability" (*LTI*, p. 15) because the conditions *warranted* an *assertion* that is always tentative to further inquiry.

Consequently, the assumptions of logical forms include: (1) inquiry changes with science knowledge and the changing problem situation, and hence logical theory will also change; (2) the subject matter of inquiry occurs operationally in the context of a problem situation; (3) logical forms are postulational to inquiry; (4) logical forms are continuous with nature; and (5) inquiry is social.

First, the story of humankind—especially since the Scientific Revolution—is the progressive discovery of the methods of science and new ways of applying those methods to create more comfort, security, and better ways of solving problems, leading to fulfillment and satisfaction in experience. Inquiry itself is also subject to adjustment and refinement.

Second, the operational determination of subject matter in inquiry proceeds in two general ways: operations upon existential materials or upon symbols. The examples Dewey provided include the practical activity of searching for a coin or constructing a balance sheet where numbers symbolize something in existence. Third, because the forms are embedded in the means-to-consequences conditions of an inquiry, they are postulational, meaning a self-evident starting point. And as a moving force in inquiry, they become a "contract" with stipulations for the inquirer to follow (*LTI*, p. 24).

The fourth assumption should be completely familiar to the reader because Dewey insisted that inquiry fit into his naturalism. As such, "there is no breach of continuity between operations of inquiry and biological operations and physical operations" and the initiation of the problematic situation "grows out of organic activities" (*LTI*, p. 26). And fifth, he acknowledges that inquiry's context is social, and the consequences will also be social with consideration especially for associated living and language.

Cumulatively, the assumptions of logical forms provide the basis for a theory of general intelligence. Dewey looked to history for guidance and concluded that humans experimented—engaged in trial-and-error—long before the Scientific Revolution. Over time, they employed logic to systematize the scientific method and locate the newly articulated and delineated method in secondary schools and research institutions. They universally recognized the success of this method and began to deploy it in art and science during the Renaissance. In fact, this marked the period where art and science parted ways (*AE*).

Dewey's unique contribution was to apply the scientific method to social spheres including areas like the work of historians. History abounds with widespread examples of individuals and groups accepting conclusions and shunning experimental thinking or prematurely terminating inquiry to embrace facts that support preconceived notions.

In effect, unsuccessful inquiry stunts the production of knowledge, and in its place ideology emerges. As Hickman (2001) noted,

> It is for this reason that even though less productive methods such as religion and magic have had some remarkable successes (defined in terms of their ability to produce satisfactory adjustment to changing conditions and to control situations that are perceived as undesirable), they have nevertheless historically proven less likely to produce such reliable results over the long haul. (p. 68)

Dewey's knowledge-production process, in contrast, is about improving methods of inquiry leading to more refined habits and better tools for acting intelligently in the world. He believed that by describing the theory and method of pragmatism, he might help move civilization away from ideological thinking or thinking based on preconceived notions.

Inquiry and Tools

Any encounter with a problem that moves into reflective consciousness becomes mediated or instrumental. The means become an instrument—a tool—for solving the problem. Depending on the type of activity, all tools are conceptual and some have material embodiment. While students may use more conceptual tools to successfully construct a DBQ essay, a carpenter may use more tangible ones such as a hammer and nails to fix a leaky roof. However, in both cases a basic thinking pattern holds because during inquiry, the tools tend to fade into the background as data emerge allowing inquirers to compare various means in the hopes of selecting the best one to affect a satisfactory conclusion.

Dewey made an astute observation that conceptual and tangible tools are roughly equal in thinking and illustrates the ebb and flow of different types of tools in the thinking process. Consequently, the student with the DBQ may employ intangible tools to analyze primary source documents like attribution, contextualization, and corroboration (Wineburg, 2001), but logically, these tools are no different than the carpenter using a hammer and nails. In the same regard, conceptual tools can fade into the background as tangible ones emerge such as a situation where the student's pen malfunctions or vice versa when the carpenter uses geometry to calculate the cut of a shingle.

In inquiry, tools are instrumental for resolving a problematic situation. They also transform *events* (i.e., past experiences) and *objects* into other things—predictive elements not in the immediacy of primary experience. Tools, therefore, are not physical extensions of humans. Dewey (*EN*) explained,

> A tool is a particular thing, but it is more than a particular thing, since it is a thing in which a connection, a sequential bond of nature is embodied. It possesses an objective relation as its own defining property. Its perception as well as its actual use takes the mind to other things. The spear suggests the feast not directly but through the medium of other external things, such as the game and the hunt, to which the sight of the weapon transports imagination. Man's bias towards himself easily leads him to think of a tool solely in relation to himself, to his hand and eyes, but its primary relationship toward other external things, as the hammer to the nail, and the plow to the soil. Only through this objective bond does it sustain a relation to man himself and his activities. A tool denotes a perception and acknowledgment of sequential bonds in nature. (pp. 123–24)

Dewey's all-encompassing perspective connects higher and lower-order beings and establishes the proper place for tools in all types of activities. Later, the logic of tools will guide the description about the use of digital tools and artifacts in learning social studies. For now, though, inquiry remains central to Dewey's system of idea about the continuity of nature, which also requires a new terminology.

A New Terminology for Old Ways of Doing and Undergoing

Dewey's naturalism highlights that all the things that society traditionally views as givens—curriculum, thinking, the work of historians, science, math, to name a few—are the connections discovered in the modern era of what humans did and underwent to evolve as humans over thousands of years. This evolutionary pathway has been documented, tested, and reaffirmed repeatedly.

In a final analysis, Dewey's premise is that the thousands of years of learning in this manner abruptly ended with the consequences of the Industrial Revolution—mass migrations to cities, factory work, separation of children from parents, child labor, the separation of labor from reflective thought, etc.—and society needed to restore awareness of these natural connections in modern schools drawing on the same successful methods and modalities of inquiry that changed humans and preserved civilization over millennia. Equally important is the idea that these methods of inquiry evolved over that time and will continue to do so with changing circumstances.

In fact, in *Democracy and Education* (1916) he argued that inquiry today is more important than before the Industrial Revolution because the problems of the Middle Ages, ancient world, and even time stretching further into the distant past demanded less critical reflection and more habitual functioning with subservience to a clan chieftain or feudal lord in exchange for basic needs and security. The modern-day equivalent is something like an army private pledging complete loyalty to the chain-of-command where the act of associated living with other privates and superiors requires more habitual-style activities than critical problem-solving ones.

In effect, the ancient Greeks devised a philosophy to fit their perceived conditions with descriptions to demarcate sharp delineations into categories such as primary and secondary substances, and that model became the Western standard until the pragmatists challenged it with science and logic. Escaping the confines of categories and constructing a philosophy continuous with nature requires a new language with phrasing to capture change and time.

Dewey forged a new vocabulary to describe the generic traits of nature such as "experience, organism/environment interaction, events, energies, relations" (Boisvert, 1988, p. 142). The new terminology encapsulates both stability and change. Live beings constantly strive for harmony and stability, which is the immediate phase following the successful resolution of a problem and lingers until the next difficulty arises. Therefore, it makes philosophical sense that the successful resolution of a problem situation with the means-end relationship represents a phase or a moment of stability as the organism adjusts into a settled state and habit assumes control until the next difficulty is perceived.

One of the conditions necessary for ontology is that the new naturalistic terminology applies to *all* beings. For example, an *event* is much more than how one employs it in common language to describe a sports competition, a treaty signing, or a birthday party. Dewey explained how events "lead an independent and double life" (*EN*, p. 166).

Accordingly, *event* is synonymous with *history*. An event remains valid as something that occurs in the past, and in the same instance, can transform into an *object* of thinking as part of inquiry. The consideration of consequences also means that events shape the future, which is what historians do or how students "do" history. The implication is that historical interpretation become themselves causes of historical change.

Inquiry as Continuous

While the new terminology may represent certain challenges for understanding Dewey, his writing style, particularly syntax, is exasperatingly confusing on the surface, but really serves a purpose (i.e., "is instrumental") for combatting anthropological bias and conveying the continuity of inquiry. A relevant example is his definition of inquiry, *"Inquiry is the controlled or directed transformation of an indeterminate situation in to one that is so determinate in its constituent distinctions and relations as to convert the elements of the original situation into a unified whole*" (*LTI*, p. 108).

What one can notice from Dewey's inquiry definition is the focus on the situation, an impersonal, passively constructed, agentless statement, which defies the conventions of engaging prose. Situations happen because nature is a serial engagement of beginnings and endings, or as Dewey wrote, "an affair *of* affairs, wherein each one, no matter how linked up it may be with others, has its *own* quality" (*EN*, p. 97). Because the directing and controlling of inquiry involves looking back with the consideration of current circumstances, and projecting toward a future denouement, inquiry is instrumental to making experience (history) continuous.

In sum, Darwin's evolution describes the *conditions* necessary for survival. These include the following: (1) Any live creature attains its ideal state following successful adaptation; (2) the surrounding conditions are always precarious and in flux; and (3) to survive, the creature either has to change itself or the surrounding conditions (Boisvert, 1988). From these, Dewey fashioned the basis for human inquiry.

From the perspective of the human being, evolution informs this process: (1) Thinking always begins with a problematic situation; (2) thinking is innate to the situation, as well as the whole person, suggesting it is not a process separate from the self like classic philosophy treated it; (3) immediate experience supplies the facts and data for resolving the problem because the problem can only exist in the existential present; (4) theory and practice are phases of our experience necessary to achieve a new harmony and equilibrium; and (5) the process of thinking is experimental.

When students "do" history, math, language arts, science, or any school subject matter, they are socially constructing meaning as our ancestors did over the course of thousands of years. To the list of words synonymous with "inquiry," one can add "do." It does not suggest that individuals who lived ten thousand years ago participated in the same types of activities because every situation is unique, and even more certainly the twists and turns to get to the present, at best, made those forebears' activities faint impressions of what came much later. The doings preceded the curriculum and the doings are the cement for continuity of experiences.

DOING THE SOCIAL STUDIES

When critics reject the instrumental nature of the social studies curriculum, they are embracing subject matter such as history and geography as fixed, a priori, permanent and unchanging and something that a mind can come to learn. Studying history for history's sake establishes a bulwark in primary experience where history can be used or enjoyed. In turn, the learner becomes a passive, knowledge recipient and the teacher is empowered to impress knowledge on the mind. The knowledge is true, unbending, and incontrovertible, and the conditions and purpose for the stamping on the mind are irrelevant.

From the instrumentalist's perspective, only inquiry activities have the potential to functionally reconstruct learners' experiences. Further, because the aim of the social studies curriculum is to create effective citizens, Dewey teaches us that these activities deliver the most impact when students have opportunities to study current social problems, which is the instrumental nature of the curriculum. At the same time, learners *use* history, geography, and other subject matter instrumentally to reconstruct their experiences.

This section examines how an inquiry approach to the social studies curriculum promotes the reconstruction of student experience. Moreover, evidence suggests that many social studies teachers struggle with two key elements of the inquiry process: integrating controversial issues and implementing effective discussion techniques. Additionally, this section examines the use of digital tools and artifacts in the social studies.

And, finally, this chapter ends with a discussion about the NCSS 3C Framework, a document to support the states' framing of the Common Core Learning Standards. In theory, the framework echoes Dewey's middle position accommodating an inquiry process while allowing individual state and local entities to determine the content. However, because politics is the ultimate instrumentalism in social affairs, what started as a widely embraced grassroots, reform effort has devolved into an aspect of the cultural wars.

Social Studies Inquiry

In a popular social studies elementary and middle levels methods textbook, Levstik and Barton (2011) ascribe the following attributes to an inquiry activity:

- There is lively conversation and intellectual negotiation among participants who each have varying degrees of expertise in the topic at hand.
- Conversation focuses on questions and tasks worthy of sustained discussion and in-depth study.
- Students use both prior knowledge and newly gathered data to "master perplexity"—to make sense out of what seemed not to make sense when their study began.
- Teachers model and students practice "classroom thoughtfulness"—taking the time necessary to think carefully and thoroughly before responding to questions or attempting to resolve problems.
- Students do history—they pose, investigate, and at least tentatively answer historical questions and develop historical explanations and interpretations—they don't just memorize the history others have done. (p. 22)

These descriptive points also contain the stages of scientific thinking, the most effective form of inquiry.

A rearrangement of the main points above yields the following statement: students with varying abilities engage in "tasks . . . [of] in-depth study . . . to resolve problems." And when they "do history—they pose" hypotheses and then "investigate" using "prior knowledge and newly gathered data" to construct knowledge leading to "historical explanations and interpretations." In addition, "conversation" and "discussion" are integral for understanding.

The complexity of the inquiry process yields three observations: First, "doing history" as a full-blown investigation is the highest form of investigation, but incremental types exist, which are also important; at the same time, all fall short of "doing social studies" because they ignore the use of intellectual tools and disciplinary concepts to interpret social events.

Second, if social problems do arise, students enact value judgments, and more likely than not, these judgments pertain to controversial issues; in fact, avoiding controversy makes an uninteresting and ineffective curriculum. And third, studies suggest that most social studies teachers struggle to facilitate effective questioning and discussion techniques.

Inquiry Is More Than Big Investigations

One interpretation why Dewey used a multiplicity of terms for inquiry is that it can mean many things in practice. In addition to things like problem-based learning or authentic intellectual work, it can also be a much less complex activity like simply asking someone who is more experienced a question or accessing a website like Wikipedia. The *Merriam-Webster Dictionary* defines inquiry as: (1) examination into facts or principles: research; (2) a request for information; and (3) a systematic investigation often of a matter of public interest (*Merriam-Webster*, 2017).

The full breadth and scope of inquiry accommodates a variety of rich classroom activities including direct instruction with engaging questioning and discussion techniques. In other words, skilled teachers use a variety of instructional strategies in a scaffolding structure to engage their students in critical thinking (i.e., reflective inquiry). At the same time, inquiry spirals throughout the curriculum because every time a student harbors a doubt and seeks out clarification, she initiates inquiry.

Digital Tools and Artifacts

During his naturalistic phase, Dewey began to describe inquiry using the term "technology" (*EN*) which is not surprising given his focus on the Greek root *techne* as the "craft," "skill," or "art" of a live creature's transaction with the world. Combined with Socrates' insistence that *techne* be combined with *logoi*, meaning "reason," "words," and "speech," the word technology emerged in the nineteenth century as an overarching designation of the inquiry process (Mitcham, 1994).

In the nineteenth century, Karl Marx was the first modern philosopher to describe technology as a subdiscipline focusing on the modes of production and their effect on social relations, and later, the German philosopher, Ernst Kapp, contrived the term "Philosophie der Technik" which translates to "Philosophy of Technology" (Mitcham, 1994; Nye, 2006).

It was not until the post–World War I era that the modern usage emerged as related to engineering and engineered products. Later, diverse schools of philosophy reacted to technology according to their critical lenses: phenomenology, positivism, and pragmatism. The phenomenology camp emphasized the habituation of technology in everyday lives; the positivists focused on the connection among science, words, logic, and truth; and philosophers in the 1970s and 1980s belatedly recognized Dewey's inquiry approach as an early pioneer in the subdiscipline (Ihde, 1993; Mitcham, 1994, 2009).

The Problem

Around the same time that philosophers were acknowledging Dewey's contributions to understanding the proper place of technology in human activity, social studies researchers began to develop an interest in how digital technologies could transform teaching and learning. Over nearly five decades, technology advocates have called for the integration of digital tools and products to enhance learning. However, investigators have consistently reported that students generally use technology in superficially cognitive ways (Beck & Eno, 2012; Combs, 2010; Shively & VanFossen, 2009; Shriner, Clark, Nail, Schlee, & Libler, 2010; Whitworth & Berson, 2002).

Keeping in mind that Dewey's lifespan began with a world lacking electricity, automobiles, and penicillin, and by his twilight years, he experienced some of the most consequential inventions of humankind like atomic energy and computers, he addressed technology in subtle and obvious ways:

> The great advance of electrical science in the last generation was closely associated, as effect and as cause, with application of electric agencies to means of communication, transportation, lighting of cities and houses, and more economical production of goods. These are *social* ends, moreover, and if they are too closely associated with notions of private profit, it is not because of anything in them but because they have been deflected to private uses:—a fact which puts upon the school the responsibility of restoring their connection, in the mind of the coming generation, with public scientific and social interests. (*DE*, pp. 151–52)

When Dewey referred to the purpose of schools in "restoring their connection . . . with public scientific and social interests" he argued that technology obscured previous connections between means and ends. For example, if a student today uses a calculator to add numbers, she does not develop the means (e.g., following the rules of addition) to arrive at the end (the sum). Instead, she uses the calculator to shortcut the manual process. In effect, technology diminishes or dissolves evolutionary connections.

What Dewey argued, in effect, is that history and geography's instrumentalism in experience is essential for restoring "the sequential bond of nature" (*EN*, p. 122) that is severed by technology's shortcuts. When placed in Dewey's philosophical framework, these observations yield the following seven guidelines for integrating digital tools and artifacts (DTAs) into the social studies curriculum:

(1) DTAs should *only* be utilized when there are clear connections to social studies aims, course goals, and lesson objectives.
(2) Working with raw materials and first hand experiences are valued over mediated experiences, particularly with young children.
(3) When engaging students with DTAs, they should already know and be proficient with the manual processes underlying electronic shortcuts.
(4) It is not enough to justify the use of DTAs because they are used authentically in the larger society, there must also be a clear connection established with student interest.
(5) DTAs embody the most potential for enhancing student learning when schools provide them with maximum of freedom and use approaching the authentic ideal.
(6) The student-teacher partnership is essential for identifying student interests, providing educative experiences, and avoiding mis-educative experiences when using DTAs.
(7) DTAs should be situated in the praxis of social studies as a content and method for promoting intelligent action. (Stuckart, 2014, pp. 64–66)

The guidelines suggest that teachers should not think of DTAs as useful merely because of a technology's affordances, but rather they should consider the interconnections among pedagogical aims, goals, and objectives.

Technology should facilitate, rather than undermine reflective thought. Younger children should have opportunities to participate manually. For example, recent evidence suggests that manual writing leads to greater cognitive growth than typing (Brewer, Damico, & Rinkevich, 2012; Hotz, 2017, April 4).

In addition to writing, many of the skills related to doing social studies—mapping, reading, graphing, and many others—require students develop manual proficiencies to truly make connections in thinking because one characteristic of intelligence is comparing means in solving a problem. In addition, teachers may want to consider offering both technology and non-technology options for completing an assignment based on individual needs and capacities.

Another issue concerning the guidelines relates to maximum freedoms. If the hardware or software is outdated, or the connections to networks are impeded, certain situations stunt student interest and create a gulf between authentic use in society and how it functions in schools. Of course, the teacher and student partnership is also a transaction with the environment requiring diligent planning and execution. And finally, technology used for inquiry in "thicker" contexts like authentic intellectual work allows for deeper multidisciplinary investigations and the reporting of results.

With the emergence of the popular internet and inexpensive computers in the 1990s, many people believed that technology would transform learning in ways that would render old ways of doing things obsolete. However, the promise of technology was never realized (Cuban, 2001) because DTAs are merely tools with the potential to act upon other objects. Dewey shows us that intelligent action involves inquiry, which is also the basis for the CCSS.

THE CURIOUS CASE OF THE COMMON CORE STATE STANDARDS

Nearly a decade ago, state and local leaders convened a national task force to produce recommendations for improving education. The recommendations later evolved into the CCSS. In the beginning, the efforts generated widespread support across the political spectrum.

However, when the Obama administration began issuing mandates, many conservatives railed about federal overreach. Around the same time, many liberals also pushed back citing the lack of research and scant input from teachers (Williams, 2014, February 27). However, if one dismisses the passionate advocacy for thoughtful analysis, the standards make sense, particularly considering Deweyan philosophy and the social studies.

To assist states with the development of their social studies standards, a broad coalition of scholars, educators, and organizations coalesced to produce the *College, Career & Civic Life C3 Framework for Social Studies State Standards* (National Council for the Social Studies, 2013). Striking a tone reminiscent of the Declaration of Independence with an incisive connection to Dewey's inquiry and how people think,

> NOW MORE THAN EVER, students need the intellectual power to recognize societal problems; ask good questions and develop robust investigations into

them; consider possible solutions and consequences; separate evidence-based claims from parochial opinions; and communicate and act upon what they learn. And most importantly, they must possess the capability and commitment to repeat that process as long as is necessary. Young people need strong tools for, and methods of, clear and disciplined thinking in order to traverse successfully the worlds of college, career, and civic life. (p. 6)

Moreover, the focus on inquiry allows individual states and districts to decide the curricular content.

The framework is composed of an inquiry arc, which supports a spiraling curriculum where students delve deeper into the content as they progress through school. With an emphasis on the subject areas of history, government, economics, and geography, states and local school districts can identify the content and skills where (1) students and teachers develop questions and plan investigations; (2) students use disciplinary concepts and tools to address social problems; (3) students have opportunities to weigh evidence, consider means and consequences, and analyze sources; and (4) communicate their findings, and engage in social action.

The C3 Framework committee also formed multiple task forces and sought feedback from numerous organizations including the Association of American Geography, American Psychological Association, and American Historical Association. By most measures, the resultant standards are rigorous. For example, by the end of high school, students are expected to "Critique the central arguments in secondary works of history on related topics in multiple media in terms of their historical accuracy" (p. 49). Despite the inclusion of ideas from many competing camps, critics abound.

The usual suspects offer sharp criticism because the new standards do not specifically list essential content (e.g., Finn Jr., 2013, September 18; Hess, 2013, September 18). As Hess (2013, September 18) remarked about the release of the framework on Constitution Day, "Now, the exercise had more than a little irony, given that the organizations went out of their way to ensure that these 'social studies standards' make no mention of the U.S. Constitution—or other historical events, dates, or persons."

These critics, however, ignore the fact that (1) the content fits within the framework and is dictated by local standards; (2) advocating the memorization of facts completely ignores the needs and capacities of the learners; and (3) social studies is already taught as history in most classrooms, and that is most likely the reason why students continue to show disinterest and why measures such as the National Association of Educational Progress' assessment of knowledge in U.S. history, geography, and civics consistently indicates that eighth-graders retain little understanding of facts and concepts (National Center for Education Statistics, 2015).

Many conservative and liberal factions oppose the CCSS and C3 Framework despite their professed beliefs in improving critical thinking, which the new standards clearly articulate. The federal-overreach and failure-to-involve-teacher-participation objections ring hollow given the myriad contradictions in their shifting positions and explanations. Dewey would have recognized these postures as political instrumentalism, suggesting that the opponents' objections are tools for desired, indirect consequences such as sound bites to incite and rally political bases. Ultimately, however, the objections may not matter because the teacher still holds the power as the curriculum gatekeeper.

SUMMARY

Inquiry is triggered when one encounters a problem that habit alone cannot resolve, and only through intelligent activity can the inquirer arrive at an acceptable conclusion. In effect, the phases of experience in inquiry include the psychical experimentation together with external contacts in the existential world. In a sense, theory (i.e., the psychical) forms a partnership with practice (i.e., purposeful movement toward a desired end). Consequently, the individual constructs knowledge in a production process as she tests means to reach a satisfying outcome.

The inquiry production process contrasts with the fixed ends of classical philosophy and involves conceptual and tangible tools. It also contrasts with curriculum and learning standards that require students learn myriad facts before engaging in their own lines of inquiry, which undermines learning and possibly underestimates student abilities.

Dewey and the other early pragmatists invented an entirely new vocabulary to capture organisms' phases of experience with a focus on change. Only humans, though, can use awareness to draw on former experiences (i.e., events) to direct intelligent activity in inquiry.

Using the content, conceptual underpinnings, and skills of the school curriculum to conduct and inform inquiry connected to contemporary social issues is *doing* the social studies. During inquiry, students reconstruct their experiences. And because the supreme goal is to improve the conditions for learning of everyone, teachers should learn how to integrate controversial public issues and effective discussion techniques. Further, in the 1970s, scholars increasingly recognized Dewey as a founder of a philosophy of technology, which also has implications for how teachers integrate technology into an inquiry curriculum.

Technology is a tool that acts as an object upon other objects. It is never purely abstract because it is always applied. Sometimes humans invent new tools, which sever natural connections. Therefore, Dewey's philosophy provides guidelines for how learners should use DTAs *naturally*, which is another way of saying that humans naturally use tools while solving problems during the inquiry process.

With a focus on inquiry, the CCSS and the NCSS C3 Framework offer the potential for a social studies curriculum with high fidelity to Deweyan ideals. The problem, however, is the same as always: as the curriculum gatekeepers, it will be up to the social studies teachers to truly implement an inquiry classroom focused on students taking informed action, which is the subject of the final chapter on citizenship.

Chapter 6

Citizenship

Focus Questions:

1 What is the purpose of a state? Publics?
2 Why should you enact a curriculum allowing students to investigate controversial public issues?
3 What elements are necessary to conduct an effective classroom discussion?

The last chapter ended with a discussion of the CCSS and the NCSS C3 Framework, a document to assist states, local school districts, and teachers in implementing social studies standards. The framework consists of four dimensions in an arc that mimics how one thinks and considers means-to-consequences (i.e., science, in Deweyan terms), with the last dimension culminating with students communicating results and engaging in social action,

> ACTIVE AND RESPONSIBLE CITIZENS identify and analyze problems; deliberate with other people about how to define and address issues; take constructive, collaborative action; reflect on their actions; create and sustain groups; and influence institutions both large and small. (National Council for the Social Studies, 2010, p. 19)

The final chapter of this work addresses the aim of the social studies, which is to encourage civic competence and active citizenship.

Despite the description above, many social studies teachers practice—perhaps even wholeheartedly embrace—a passive citizenship model where students are receivers of custom and information (Barr et al., 1978; Ochoa-Becker, 1996). Given the competing demands of the classroom together with the overlapping, contradictory mandates of districts and schools, returning to Dewey's fold may help the field find coherence.

The main theme of this work is Dewey's contention that the most vital role of education is to promote the *habit* of intelligent activity in young people. And because the United States is a richly diverse, pluralistic nation, Dewey's philosophy looks to democracy as the ideal political system for unleashing the individual's power for intelligent activity, or as Westbrook (1991) remarks, "Individuals could realize themselves only as members of a community, and only those who did so were truly free" (p. 44).

Democracy, therefore, is more than a political organization, and instead becomes *an active process* where the individual strives for maximum growth and satisfaction. And much like a person reconstructs herself in the face of a problematic situation groups of citizens do the same in the face of a problematic society. Therefore, in Dewey's broad definition, democracy is synonymous with problem solving and "conjoint communicated experience" (*DE*, p. 68).

A vision for social studies teachers is to enact a curriculum where students have multiple opportunities to study current social problems and divergent viewpoints, propose solutions, and then act on those solutions; promote student involvement in extracurricular organizations; and contribute to a school-wide democratic culture.

DEWEY'S DEMOCRACY

Dewey's radical, liberal democracy stood in stark contrast to the xenophobic assimilation coursing through politics in the beginning decades of the 1900s resulting in outcomes like the Red Scare and The Immigration Act of 1924. Grounded in human transactions, Dewey articulated a liberal vision where individuals formed *publics* based on shared interests and desires.

These associations were not only vital for satisfying personal wants, but were also necessary for maintaining democracy in a socially interdependent country with a diverse citizenry. In fact, Dewey believed that a person's participation in publics should be encouraged and nurtured with the freedom of movement and self-expression. As he pointed out, "Associated or joint activity is a condition of the creation of a community. But association itself is physical and organic, while communal life is moral, that is emotionally, intellectually, consciously sustained" (*PP*, p. 151).

Social Naturalism

As with all Deweyan philosophy, the origins of citizenship and democracy are firmly planted in evolution and human interactions with natural objects including other human beings. Moreover, the consequences of these actions form the conditions for "associated living" (*DE*, p. 68), and when combined with the uniquely human trait of using intelligence to surmount hesitation, doubt, and indeterminate situations, they result in the control of means to affect consequences. In sum, only humans consciously use intelligence to either guide a situation toward desirable consequences or away from undesirable ones.

Society, then, consists of individuals trying to make sense of the world at the same time. As individuals form judgments and then act on those judgments, they affect those around them, and sometimes, they touch people who are not immediately part of the situation. In a familiar pattern, Dewey redefined "the state," rejecting a traditional definition like a circumscribed geographical area with a politically united citizenry in favor of an instrumental definition.

The State as Instrument

In a series of lectures delivered in the late 1920s, and shortly thereafter edited and collected in his work, *The Public and Its Problems* (1927), Dewey posited that the "nature of the state" flowed from "the enduring and extensive consequences of behavior, which like all behavior proceeds in ultimate analysis through individual human beings" (p. 17). Ensconced in human activity, he further advanced that the behavior of individuals resulted in direct and indirect consequences:

> In this distinction we find the germ of the distinction between the private and the public. When indirect consequences are recognized and there is effort to regulate them, something having the traits of a state comes into existence. When the consequences of an action are confined, or are thought to be confined, mainly to the persons directly engaged in it, the transaction is a private one. (*PP*, pp. 12–13)

In his distinctions, then, the state emerges as *an instrument* to regulate the actions of individuals or groups of individuals to either prevent harm or to promote the social good.

When the consequences of private behavior indirectly affect others, it becomes a public matter requiring regulation. Therefore, Dewey defined *public* as "all those who are affected by the indirect consequences of transactions to such an extent that it is deemed necessary to have those consequences systematically cared for" (p. 16). That is to say, publics allow the indirectly affected individuals in society to "act through suitable structures" and "organize ... for oversight and regulation" (pp. 28–29). Accordingly, one should not think of *the* public in the vernacular as a unified citizenry, but rather as multiple, overlapping *publics* where individuals associate with others in many different types of configurations forming what one might call civil society.

An individual may join a local synagogue, mosque, or church and be part of a religious public, and at the same time, participate in other publics like a trade union, bowling league, political party, and a veterans group. Every public is a moral association of like-minded persons and exists because of the shared interests of its members, but fundamentally it is constituted of individuals and their perceptions:

> The consequences of conjoint action take on a new value when they are observed. For notice of the effects of connected action forces men to reflect upon the connection itself; it makes it an object of attention and interest. Each [person] acts, in so far as the connection is known, in view of the connection. Individuals still do the thinking, desiring and purposing, but *what* they think of is the consequences of their behavior upon that of others and that of others upon themselves. (*PP*, p. 24)

The last part is also the basis for his moral theory (see chapter 4). In much the same way as adults, young people also identify with publics in schools and communities.

Young Persons' Publics

Adults expect young people to become "well-rounded individuals." In fact, many colleges make admission decisions based on an applicant's participation in voluntary organizations. Students join debate teams, play in bands, participate in basketball squads, and volunteer at hospitals and daycare centers. These extracurricular activities become part of the miniature societies replicated across thousands of places preparing young people for participation in the wider community.

Parker (2003) identifies three ways that voluntary organizations contribute to young people's citizenship identity. First, organizations expose students to diverse perspectives beyond their own family connections. An individual student offers her perspective to others, and a pluralist collection of perspectives forms. In turn, each student can view and analyze her own unique perspective across a wider social backdrop, revealing differences, discord, and harmony beyond one's own family structure as "the idiosyncrasy of one's family life can be seen in the reflective mirror of a broadened social horizon, and pluralism becomes—to some degree—a fact in one's own life" (p. 39).

Second, in a social inquiry activity, students are also exposed to problems beyond their families, and the pluralist perspectives transform into social *tools*. Although social science approach advocates tend to reject the elementary social studies expanding horizons curriculum, Dewey would argue that no matter what comprises the local curriculum content, the central idea is still that young people continue to tackle problems beyond the spheres of their immediate families, which necessarily involves a history-rich curriculum (Wade, 2002).

Moreover, because solving a problem involves intelligence and the inner experimentation of reflecting on consequences, the student's arsenal of tools expands allowing her to consider how the consequences affect others. In Dewey's reconstructivist theory, social tools are the most precious and effective type of tools, requiring careful tending and maintenance, so the goal is "to educate the individual and diversify the social milieu so that these tools will be brought into question (a bottom-up/indeterminate approach)" (Glassman, 2001, p. 6).

Third, students in voluntary organizations learn the proper social norms for participation, including settling differences and ensuring the survival of the group. The norms will differ among organizations over time and place. In a student council organization, students may follow Robert's Rules of Order, but on a hockey team they may use less structured tactics such as direct and blunt conversation to initiate conflict resolution, "still socially sanctioned conduct proceeds at full steam, decisions get made, and the group's future is not put at risk" (Parker, 2003, p. 40).

Publics, Officials, and Government

Sometimes the interests of the members of various organizations align and the decisions of its leaders and members create indirect consequences that benefit many constituents. At other times, a seemingly benign move such as scheduling a charity event in a gymnasium can lead to an indirect consequence such as a girls' basketball team losing the opportunity to host a game. Subsequently, *officials* are charged with the task of attending to consequences.

The logic of publics begins with the premise that humans evolve through associated living and adaptation, which inherently suggests conjoint actions are infused into the process. Humans retain the traits and habits of those who came before, and in fact, can only survive and thrive with cooperative action. When individuals who are indirectly affected reflect on the consequences of these actions, they generate common interests with "purposes, plans, measures and means, to secure consequences which are liked and eliminate those which are found obnoxious" (*PP*, p. 34).

These individuals share common interests and organically form publics. When the officials charged with regulating the consequences such as "guardians of custom, as legislators, as executives, judges, etc." are political in nature, they go by the name of *government*. Government, then, comprises only the officials and differs from the state, which includes both the officials and the publics.

Publics and Democracy

Although Dewey wrote about democracy beginning in the latter half of the nineteenth century, and undoubtedly his most famous work on the topic is *Democracy and Education* (1916), he did not reach his zenith for explicating a vision of radical, liberal democracy until the publication of *The Public and Its Problems* (1927). For Dewey, "The Public" (p. 35) represented a bulwark of democracy because he not only held an unshakeable faith in individuals' abilities to elect governing officials, but also a belief in the power of citizens to discover and rally around common interests and then make decisions.

Dewey's democracy originates in the grassroots associations and interpersonal relationships of publics, which allowed him to craft an explanation transcending an atomistic view of disconnected citizens clamoring for their individual interests. These publics represent the dynamic arenas, "the permanent space of contingency in the sense that there can be no *a priori* delimitation, except as it emerges from individuals and groups that coalesce in the service of problem solving" (Rogers, 2012, p. 14).

Overlapping publics comprise the fabric of civil society. Conversely, inchoate associations become publics precisely because tensions flare among them:

> In civil society, information and pressures are communicated across those associations. In such pluralistic conditions, problems and conflicts are bound to emerge; some of these may very well come from the functioning of governmental regulation or activities of the market economy. The result of such problems is that groups within civil society are politicized so become a public. (Rogers, 2012, pp. 24–25)

The publics function as a pressure valve where problems and indeterminate situations unite individuals into common interest associations because other principles indirectly affect them.

This is the space where unity and differences collide, multiple perspectives are contributed, proposed solutions deliberated, and a way forward identified. The publics are not instrumental for solving the problem because their functioning is raw, direct, indeterminate, and in flux. Only the emergence of the state with its full breadth of instrumentalities can make an indeterminate situation be transformed into a determinate status. As Westbrook (1991) notes,

> The state ... was simply a mechanism for mediating the conflicts between the groups in a society. Groups existed prior to the state, and the state was but an instrument for adjudicating the disputes arising among them. The state ... was not an absolute power absorbing all the interests in a society, and to conceive of it as such was to threaten social freedom." (p. 246)

The only way that democracy can work and states achieve a measure of instrumentality is for public officials to be receptive and responsive to the publics, that is, to be continuous with them and act as public servants.

The state comprises both officials and members of the public, and Dewey offered criteria for measuring a state's effectiveness, "the degree of organization of the public which is attained, and the degree in which its officers are so constituted as to perform their function of caring for public interests" (*PP*, p. 33). In a sense, the public officials become experts in their specific domains whether they serve as judges, mayors, cabinet secretaries, or any other position for regulating the indirect consequences of associated living.

Public Officials as Experts

Democracy thrives in the interstices between the political experts and the citizenry. Dewey's central argument was that the experts can only solve problems with hypotheses that are framed from the problems themselves. Consequently, "even such rudimentary political forms as democracy . . . to some extent involve a consultation and discussion which uncover social needs and problems" (*PP*, p. 206). And because the problems drive the methods, "they imply the existence of a complex horizon of value and meaning that is now fractured and in need of creative valuation to restore continuity" (Rogers, 2012, p. 20)

At a time when democracy was under assault because of the perceived failure of the masses to recognize pro-war propaganda, which translated into enthusiastic support for entry into World War I, Dewey offered an unapologetic rebuttal to members of the 1920s intelligentsia who argued for an expert class of officials operating independently of the people. For that reason, Dewey famously wrote, "The man who wears the shoe knows best that it pinches and where it pinches, even if the expert shoemaker is the best judge of how that trouble is to be remedied" (*PP*, p. 207).

Dewey suggested that the shoemaker might be able to fix a pinch, but without the input of the wearer, she or he will not be able to embark on the best method for doing so. In the final chapter of *The Public and Its Problems* (1927), "The Problem of Method," Dewey explicated how citizens and experts interact in a liberal democracy. First, as the shoemaker analogy illustrates, problems manifest at the community level, obstructing individuals from exercising their freedoms to live their lives to their potential.

Second, Dewey entrusted free inquiry to lead to solutions that will allow individuals to enlarge their experiences, leading to more growth and development:

> Scientific thinking entailed not only the use of a particular method but participation in a community possessed of specific cognitive virtues, and Dewey

believed these virtues—free inquiry, toleration of diverse opinion, and free communication—were necessary if not sufficient attributes of a democratic society and polity. (Westbrook, 1991, p. 170)

And third, Dewey's ethics required that the resolution of difficulties must consider how the resolution affects others and this can only occur with communication.

Authority flows from the problems and concerns of the masses (i.e., the indeterminate situation) to the expert officials who jointly exercise power as the *state* (i.e., the instrument). Therefore, the experts can only be *expert* because the people engage in deliberations within and across their publics. The deliberations also include disagreements over who the experts are at a given time, further undercutting the 1920s elites who argued for a permanent, expert class of rulers (Rogers, 2012).

Because the purpose of rulers is to regulate the few to benefit the many, Dewey insisted that expert officials were susceptible to corruption. Certainly today, we should be suspect of our politicians who must raise vast sums of money from private interests to finance modern campaigns, particularly when unlimited amounts of money flow without any type of oversight or transparency as "dark money." It is fair to deduce that some officials are making judgments to benefit their wealthy benefactors at the expense of the common citizens.

Therefore, publics not only support the state in rendering judgments, they also serve as a sort of check on power; they demand openness in how their officials conduct business; they contest decisions perceived as unfair; and they supply the data for contingency because environing conditions are always changing and the best decision yesterday may not be the best one for today or even tomorrow.

Public Problems

After carefully weaving his narrative, Dewey illuminated the problem of the public near the end of the final chapter, "The essential need, in other words, is the improvement of the methods and conditions of debate, discussion and persuasion. That is *the* problem of the public" (*PP*, p. 208). In other words, social inquiry and deliberation are at the heart of democracy.

American liberal democracy hatched from small-town communal life, and was later eclipsed by the forces of modern social change into what Dewey described as the "Great Society" (*PP*, p. 157), where "the non-political forces are expressions of a technological age injected into an inherited political scheme which operates to deflect and distort their normal operation" (*PP*, p. 129).

Many people are disillusioned today—as they were in the 1920s—because these vast social changes are a consequence of globalization, which makes Dewey's observation still relevant from nearly a century ago, "The local communities without intent or forecast found their affairs conditioned by remote and invisible organization" (p. 98). For example, the nature of work has never been more dependent on global conditions as it is today, and many people feel powerless to control their own destinies.

THE SOCIAL STUDIES

The founders of the social studies embarked on a curriculum experiment and parted ways with the traditional academic disciplines. Jettisoning the idea that students should learn history for history's sake, the social studies offers a purpose to improve the conditions for all with a clear focus on democratic values and virtues. In the classroom, this translates into two critical elements that are either absent or the teacher poorly executes them: giving students opportunities to study public issues and meaningful discussions.

Controversial Public Issues

Since the inception of the social studies curriculum over a century ago, advocates have called for the study of controversial public issues (CPI), which they have also called taboo topics, issues-centered curriculum, and many similar names (Hunt & Metcalf, 1955; Newmann, 1975; Newmann & Oliver, 1970; Rugg, 1939). The central characteristic of CPI is the focus on problems in a democratic society where citizens perceive conflicting values.

Given the massive social displacements evident in the beginning of the twentieth century, one of the first approaches was a course of study, problems of democracy (Evans, 2010). Later in the 1960s and reflecting the context of that period, students and teachers adapted a legal lens to study controversy and change. Over the past couple decades, many social studies advocates have called for the inclusion of CPI, which is especially salient today given how politically polarized U.S. politics has become (Hess, 2008).

However, many teachers avoid CPI in their classrooms for a variety of reasons despite the clear connections between value conflicts and active citizenship. New teachers avoid them because they are concerned with angry reactions from parents and administrators, and the possibility of losing their teaching appointments. Experienced teachers express concern with losing control over classroom management and maintaining harmony among students. Evidence also suggests that teachers disagree about what makes an issue controversial (Alongi, 2016; Hess, 2002; Tannebaum, 2013; Washington & Humphries, 2011).

Refining Your Rationale with CPI and Local Values

Nearly all social studies teachers agree in the purpose of the social studies for promoting citizenship, but may differ in exactly what that means. Therefore, in this final chapter, teachers can refine their rationales in the context of CPI (Ochoa-Becker, 1996; Shaver, 1977). Ochoa-Becker (1996) points out that if democracy is to flourish, educators must break away from chronological history pedagogy and develop a "curriculum [that] emphasizes the issues that citizens persistently face—from those concerning the environment to issues of pluralism and distribution of wealth—using the social science disciplines, where appropriate, to substantially deepen student understanding" (pp. 6–7).

To reflect local values and promote acceptance, stakeholders—including teachers, school leaders, members of the local education board, and community members—should draft a rationale for studying CPI. Further, including CPI does not necessarily mean a liberal approach to problem solving because the framework can include all political viewpoints and courses of action (Evans, Newmann, & Saxe, 1996). Moreover, the rationale should be constructed and considered a dynamic and flexible statement of goals that is sensitive to changing conditions (Ochoa-Becker, 1996).

Building a CPI Curriculum

While the rationale can help frame the building of the CPI curriculum, the building itself should be deliberative and involve several steps. The purpose is for students to engage in deep study about conflicting, persistent issues, not to merely express prejudices and biases (i.e., share their opinions about something), but to research various positions and arrive at a reasoned belief. Four principles to consider include

> first, depth of understanding is more important than coverage and superficial exposure.... Second, topics and issues need to be connected through some kind of thematic, disciplinary, interdisciplinary, or historical structure.... Third, as indicated in the definition, the study of issues must be substantially grounded in challenging content.... Fourth, students must experience influence and control in the inquiry process. (Evans et al., 1996, p. 3)

These principles also mirror the development of a CCSS approach to learning social studies.

Unlike content standards that often lead to high-stakes tests where students regurgitate the "correct" answer, the social studies CCSS emphasize the weighing of evidence, the construction of reasoned and logical responses, and extended written and sometimes oral responses. According to Evans et al. (1996), the unique social milieu of every classroom may dictate the approach, but in general,

> first, issues must take the form of truly problematic questions, even for the teacher. . . . Second, in working out well-reasoned positions on issues, students will need access to a variety of resources and tools that extend beyond the teacher and the classic textbooks. . . . Third, students need continuous practice in using extended oral and written language. . . . Fourth, a major pedagogical challenge for teachers is to learn how to help students feel comfortable with the cognitive ambiguity that issues-centered education introduces. (p. 4)

Providing students opportunities to study social problems does not necessarily threaten a teacher's worldview about the proper role of history education.

Instead, teachers create a CPI curriculum to prepare students in becoming full members in a democratic society. As Hess (2008) summarized,

> Teachers' beliefs about what constitutes an issue, what issues should be included in the curriculum, and whether they should disclose their own views, illustrates that most teachers do not include issues in the curriculum because they want to indoctrinate students into a particular point of view. Instead, they seek a way to engage students in talking about their own views within the bounds of community norms. (p. 130)

The author also reports that students who engage with CPI show a deeper understanding of social studies content, become more politically active, and enhance their democratic values in areas such as tolerance.

Enacting a PPD Curriculum

Parker (2003) suggested a one-semester course, public policy deliberation (PPD), which would combine CPI and a new and relevant version of the old, 1916 course, problems of democracy. Acknowledging the overburdened curriculum, he argued that democracy is too important and extraordinarily difficult to maintain to not attempt a new course with three parts (although Dewey (1946) would not agree because he publicly stated that the curriculum was too expansive and teachers already should be addressing these types of deliberations across all content areas).

The first part asks students to identify and explain a public problem while signifying the stakeholders and their positions. The second part requires that they create and analyze policy options, including the opportunity costs associated with choosing one over another. And third, they must decide and justify what actions to take. Building on the original problem of democracy guidelines, the author presented the following criteria for problem selection:

1. Interest: select problems in which students are or are likely (with coaching, knowledge, and experience) to become interested.
2. Authenticity: select genuine public problems, ones that an identifiable public (locally, nationally, internationally) is actually facing.
3. Value conflict: select problems in which value conflicts are vivid so as to encourage value analysis throughout the model (i.e., the needed policy choice requires students to examine alternatives that express diverse and competing values).
4. Pluralism: select problems in which the pluralistic nature of American society is evident (i.e., there are multiple and competing cultural and political perspectives on the issue and, therefore, the opportunity to adjudicate competing perspectives).
5. Perenniality: select problems for which analogous cases are available so as to encourage cross-case comparison. The immediate policy question should be an instance of an enduring public problem that publics across time and place have had to face.
6. Curriculum materials: select problems for which thoughtfully prepared instructional resources are already available. (Parker, 2003, p. 122)

Further, a key feature of CPI involves democratic discourse, something Dewey believed was lacking because of the vast social changes of the modern age.

Discussion

Dewey's thesis is that the intricacies of the modern world results in a "Great Society" at the expense of local citizens coming together to civically participate—presenting their perspectives, twisting arms, explicating concerns, resolving differences face-to-face, and devising solutions in a more-or-less respectful and direct fashion (notwithstanding who could participate throughout time and place). Accordingly, the problem of the public is to figure out a way to promote a "Great Community" (*PP*, p. 157) based on mutual respect for differing opinions, and in effect, result in concerned citizens' willingness to change their beliefs.

Effective, democratic discussion techniques must be the foundation for the social studies to achieve effective citizenship. However, after a century of implementation efforts three consequences are clear: One, facilitating effective discussion is challenging and difficult. Two, discussions occur much less frequently than both students and teachers say they do. And three, despite many schools being organized along class and color lines (Banks & Banks,

2010), schools still represent the best societal opportunities for coming into contact with diverse perspectives (Parker, 2003).

Hess (2010) provides one of the most authoritative accounts linking controversial issues with democratic discourse. After considering several definitions of discussion, she provides two characteristics that all have in common. First, she recognizes that discussion must include an actual conversation among two or more people with an exchange of some type of content. Second, she posits that the exchange sparks a building process and can potentially result in a net positive for the participants. In other words, those who engage in discussion can enhance their understanding as an outcome of the experience.

In addition to learning the social studies content in a sustained fashion, students also benefit from discussion in several additional ways. The process allows participants to experiment with ideas and consider deeper meanings as they analyze competing claims and weigh the evidence. Further, discussion also provides students the opportunity to practice strategies to resolve differences. Despite some community's efforts to segregate students using de facto methods such as tracking, most schools are much more diverse than other social institutions providing rare opportunities for diverse populations to come into contact.

One of the main benefits of controversial issues and discussion is that students enjoy interacting with others. Young people can explore their interests related to a variety of topics. As one group of researchers commented, "The sense that something is wrong is compelling, especially to adolescents who are already developing their own critiques of the world" (Kahne & Westheimer, 2006, p. 306).

Just as there is no universal definition of discussion, Hess (2010) also remarks that the characteristics also differ among experts. She does, however, offer seven aspects for social studies teachers to consider:

1. Focus on an interpretable text, issue, idea, and so on.
2. The facilitator and participants have prepared thoroughly.
3. Most of the talk comes from the participants, not the facilitator.
4. There is enough time spent on a particular idea to explore it thoroughly before going to another point.
5. Participants feel comfortable, but there is still meaningful argument.
6. Many people talk.
7. Participants and facilitator ask authentic questions and refer to previous points made in the discussion. (p. 210)

Being a teacher facilitator and a student participant requires great skill and most likely will take time to develop.

Democracy in Schools

A vision for social studies teachers is to facilitate diverse student activities in the classroom, and at the same time, to actively promote a democratic school with shared decision making, truly integrated class structures, and the creation and maintenance of organizations where students from every background can voluntarily come together and explore their shared interests. In Dewey's philosophy, diversity is a potent tool in the reconstruction of experience.

A cornerstone of the historian's reconstruction of an event is equivalent to a learner's reconstruction of experience to surmount an obstacle or difficulty. In both cases, the inquirer engages with multiple perspectives to arrive at a judgment resulting in a settled belief. For the historian, the perspectives are tools for constructing a viable interpretation.

For the learner, the more diverse perspectives she encounters, engages with, and reflects upon, the sharper her arsenal becomes for solving problems and enlarging her experiences. The goal, then, is to expand and enrich the diversity stew in schools—not just to place more diverse students in schools, but to also promote meaningful interactions within classrooms and across campus. Ochoa-Becker (2007) suggested the following school-wide practices:

- Treating each individual with respect and care on a consistent basis.
- Engaging student councils and student courts in handling issues of school and classroom discipline in ways that are taken seriously. They must not serve as window dressing.
- Modeling behavior by teachers and administrators that is consistent with respect for pluralism, with diverse student-citizens and professionals. They need to see to it that both the school and its curriculum visibly demonstrate attention to diversity, including gender as well as issues, influencing the entire global community.
- Encouraging faculty, staff, and student-citizen involvement to design democratic practices for school and classroom management.
- Encouraging both teachers and student-citizens to plan together to develop constructive conditions for teaching and learning and to generate criteria for assessment and evaluation policies mutually.
- Providing resources that support investigation of multiple sources for understanding and taking a defensible position regarding controversial issues (both print and technological), facilitating relevant classroom speakers, as well as field trips.
- Communicating with and involving parents in the development of curriculum and school practices.

- Involving parents, school boards, teachers, and student-citizens in the design and implementation of academic freedom policies and procedures.
- Establishing the position of Community Counselor, who is a teacher who can guide and arrange social action and service learning experiences, handle seminars where young citizens give serious consideration to the meaning of their community experiences and analyze them for their effectiveness. (pp. 294–95)

None of these strategies are easy because humans are not naturally predisposed to democracy.

In Dewey's philosophy, however, democracy is *instrumental* because it indirectly benefits the individual by improving the conditions for intelligence. As Dewey (*EE*) proclaimed, "The only freedom that is of enduring importance is freedom of intelligence, that is to say, freedom of observation and of judgment exercised in behalf of purposes that are intrinsically worth while" (p. 61). By ignoring student interests and feeding them information to memorize in place of conducting *social studies* of public issues, teachers are subsuming an evolutionary process of how people think.

Dewey's philosophy is comprehensively inclusive. Citizenship Transmission Teachers should recognize their beliefs as data points equivalent to the curriculum's content items, and analogous to Dewey's advocacy for viewing the fixed aspects of traditional customs and morals as a resource, not an end. The social studies teacher must begin with a careful analysis of her or his own beliefs and be willing to approach the students and subject matter with open-mindedness, wholeheartedness, and a democratic spirit.

SUMMARY

Given the central aim of the social studies in preparing young people for democratic citizenship, a remark attributed to the late philosopher, Richard Rorty, seems apt, "At the end of every blind alley we seem to find Dewey" (Berube, 2010, p. v). Dewey was a pioneer in so many educational areas, but he will always rank as the staunchest promoter of democracy, education, and citizenship.

Dewey's radical democracy conceives the state in terms of an instrument to regulate consequences and articulates the conjoint activities of citizens as the true wealth of the nation. The activities are vibrant because people follow their interests, and they are enriched with the bounty of diversity in a pluralistic society. Dewey spent most of his adult life arguing that, as miniature societies, only schools can effectively inculcate democratic values in young people.

Founded on these principles, the social studies field has always promoted the studying of social problems in schools. Further, given the complexity of most issues, the process is only effective if the teacher develops the expertise to conduct meaningful discussions. Unfortunately, research shows that most teachers avoid controversy and most also do not employ impactful discussion techniques. A vision for social studies is to perfect these skills and perpetually promote democracy and democratic processes.

References

Adler, S. (1994). Reflective practice and teacher education. In E. W. Ross (Ed.), *Reflective Practice in Social Studies* (pp. 51–8). Washington, DC: National Council for the Social Studies.

Adler, S. A. (1991). The education of social studies teachers. In J. P. Shaver (Ed.), *Handbook of Research on Social Studies Teaching and Learning* (pp. 210–21). New York: Macmillan Publishing Company.

Alongi, M. D. (2016). Real-world engagement with controversial issues in history and social studies: Teaching for transformative experiences and conceptual change. *Journal of Social Science Education 15*(2), 26–41. doi:10.4119/UNIBI/jsse-v15-i2–1479.

Anderson, D., & Cook, T. (2014). Committed to differentiation and engagement: A case study of two American secondary social studies teachers. *Journal of Social Studies Education Research 5*(1), 1–19.

Anderson, E. (2014). Dewey's moral philosophy. In E. N. Zalta (Ed.), *The Stanford Encyclopedia of Philosophy*. Stanford, CA: Metaphysics Research Lab, Stanford University. Retrieved from https://plato.stanford.edu/entries/dewey-moral/

Anton, J. (1965). John Dewey and ancient philosophies. *Philosophy and Phenomenological Research 25*(4), 477–99.

Austin, E. H. (1965). Dewey's consistent attitude toward history. *Educational Theory 15*, 198–204.

Bai, H., & Ertmer, P. A. (2008). Teacher educators' beliefs and technology uses as predictors of preservice teachers' beliefs and technology attitudes. *Journal of Technology and Teacher Education 16*(1), 93–112.

Banks, J. A., & Banks, C. A. M. (Eds.). (2010). *Multicultural Education: Issues and Perspectives* (7th ed.). Hoboken, NJ: John Wiley & Sons, Inc.

Barr, R., Barth, J. L., & Shermis, S. S. (1978). *The Nature of the Social Studies*. Palm Springs, CA: ETC Publications.

Barth, J. L., & Shermis, S. S. (1970). Defining the social studies: An exploration of three traditions. *Social Education 34*(8), 743–51.

Barton, K. C., & Levstik, L. S. (2004). *Teaching History for the Common Good*. Mahwah, NJ: Lawrence Erlbaum Associates.

Beck, D., & Eno, J. (2012). Signature pedagogy: A literature review of social studies technology and research. *Computers in the Schools 29*(1–2), 70–94. doi:10.1080/07380569.2012.658347.

Berube, M. (2010). Foreword. In D. W. Stuckart & J. Glanz (Eds.), *Revisiting Dewey: Best Practices for Educating the Whole Child Today* (pp. v–vi). Lanham, MD: Rowman & Littlefield Education.

Blau, J. L. (1960). John Dewey's theory of history. *The Journal of Philosophy LVII*(3), 89–100.

Boisvert, R. D. (1988). *Dewey's Metaphysics*. New York: Fordham University Press.

Bondy, E., Ross, D., Adams, A., Nowak, R., Brownell, M., & Hoppey, D. (2007). Personal epistemologies and learning to teach. *Teacher Education and Special Education 30*(2), 67–82.

Boydston, J. A. (1992/1993). The Dewey Center and the collected works of John Dewey. *Free Inquiry 13*(1), 19–24.

Brewer, H., Damico, J., & Rinkevich, J. (2012). Enhancing core skills outside of the traditional core curriculum: The biological, physical, and visual and what they mean to literacy. *National Teacher Education Journal 5*(2), 5–14.

Bruner, J. (1977). *The Process of Education*. Cambridge, MA: Harvard University Press.

Carmody, R. N., Weintraub, G. S., & Wrangham, R. W. (2011). Energetic consequences of thermal and nonthermal food processing. *Proceedings of the National Academy of Sciences in the United States of America 108*(48), 19199–203.

Caron, E. (2004). The impact of a methods course on teaching practices: Implementing issues-centered teaching in the secondary social studies classroom. *Journal of Social Studies Research 28*(2), 4–19.

Combs, H. J. (2010). Instructional technology: Status in middle and high school social studies. *National Teacher Education Journal 3*(3), 23–31.

Cremin, L. A. (1959). John Dewey and the Progressive-Education Movement, 1915–1952. *The School Review 67*(2), 160–73.

Cuban, L. (2001). *Oversold and Underused: Computers in the Classroom*. Cambridge, MA: Harvard University Press.

Cubberley, E. P. (1947). *Public Education in the United States: A Study and Interpretation of American Educational History*. New York: Houghton Mifflin Company.

Darling, J. (1994). *Child-Centered Education and Its Critics*. London: Paul Chapman Publishing Ltd.

Darling-Hammond, L. (2000). How teacher education matters. *Journal of Teacher Education 51*(3), 166–73.

Deci, E. L., & Ryan, R. M. (1985). *Intrinsic Motivation and Self-Determination in Human Behavior*. New York: Plenum Press.

Dewey, J. (1910). *How We Think*. New York: D. C. Heath & Company, Publishers.

Dewey, J. (1913). *Interest and Effort in Education*. New York: Houghton Mifflin Company.

Dewey, J. (1920). *Reconstruction in Philosophy*. New York: Henry Holt and Company.

Dewey, J. (1922). *Human Nature and Conduct: An Introduction to Social Psychology*. New York: Henry Holt and Company.

Dewey, J. (1929). *The Quest for Certainty: A Study of the Relation of Knowledge and Action*. New York: Minton, Balch & Company.
Dewey, J. (1938). *Experience and Education*. New York: The Macmillan Company.
Dewey, J. (1939). Theory of valuation. In O. Neurath, R. Carnap, & C. W. Morris (Eds.), *International Encyclopedia of Unified Science* (Vol. II, pp. 1–67). Chicago, IL: University of Chicago Press.
Dewey, J. (1946). What is social study? *Problems of Men* (pp. 180–83). New York: Philosophical Library.
Dewey, J. (1954). *The Public and Its Problems*. Athens, OH: Swallow Press. (Original work published 1927)
Dewey, J. (1958). *Experience and Nature*. London: George Allen & Unwin, Ltd. (Original work published 1929)
Dewey, J. (1984). The development of American Pragmatism. In J. A. Boydston (Ed.), *John Dewey: The Later Works, 1925–1953* (Vol. 2, pp. 3–21). Carbondale, IL: Southern Illinois University Press.
Dewey, J. (1991). Logic: The theory of inquiry. In J. A. Boydston (Ed.), *John Dewey: The Later Works, 1925–1953* (Vol. 12, pp. 1–549). Carbondale, IL: Southern Illinois University Press.
Dewey, J. (1996). *Theory of the Moral Life*. New York: Irvington Publishers, Inc. (Original work published 1932)
Dewey, J. (2001). *The School and Society & the Child and the Curriculum*. Mineola, NY: Dover Publications, Inc. (Original work published 1900) (Original work published 1902)
Dewey, J. (2005). *Art as Experience*. New York: Penguin Group, Inc. (Original work published 1934)
Dewey, J. (2007). *Democracy and Education*. Middlesex, U.K.: The Echo Library. (Original work published 1916)
Dewey, J. (2008). The challenge of democracy to education. In J. A. Boydston (Ed.), *John Dewey: The Later Works, 1935–1937* (Vol. 11, pp. 181–90). Carbondale, IL: Southern Illinois University Press.
Diamond, J. (1997). *Guns, Germs and Steel: The Fates of Human Societies*. New York: W. W. Norton & Company.
Dinkelman, T. (1999). Critical reflection in a social studies methods semester. *Theory and Research in Social Education 27*(3), 329–57.
Dinkelman, T. (2009). Reflection and resistance: The challenge of rationale-based teacher education. *Journal of Inquiry and Action in Education 2*(1), 91–108.
Dykhuizen, G. (1959). John Dewey: The Vermont years. *Journal of the History of Ideas 20*(4), 515–44.
Egan, K. (1980). John Dewey and the Social Studies Curriculum. *Theory and Research in Social Education 8*(2), 37–55.
Egan, K. (1983). Social studies and the erosion of education. *Curriculum Inquiry 13*(2), 195–214.
Elby, A., & Hammer, D. (2010). Epistemological resources for framing: A cognitive framework for helping teachers interpret and respond to their students' epistemologies. In L. D. Bendixen & F. C. Feucht (Eds.), *Personal Epistemology in the Classroom: Theory, Research, and Implications for Practice* (pp. 409–34). Cambridge, U.K.: Cambridge University Press.

Engle, S. H. (1960). Decision making: The heart of social studies instruction. *Social Education 24*(7), 301–306.

Engle, S. H., & Ochoa-Becker, A. S. (1988). *Educating Citizens for Democracy: Decision Making in Social Studies.* New York: Teachers College Press.

Erickson, H. L. (2008). *Stirring the Head, Heart, and Soul: Redefining Curriculum, Instruction, and Concept-Based Learning* (3rd ed.). Thousand Oaks, CA: Corwin Press.

Evans, R. W. (2004). *The Social Studies Wars: What Should We Teach the Children?* New York: Teachers College Press.

Evans, R. W. (2010). The social studies wars, now and then. In W. C. Parker (Ed.), *Social Studies Today: Research and Practice* (pp. 25–34). New York: Routledge.

Evans, R. W., Newmann, F. M., & Saxe, D. W. (1996). Defining issues-centered education. In R. W. Evans & D. W. Saxe (Eds.), *Handbook on Teaching Social Issues. NCSS Bulletin 93* (pp. 2–5). Washington, DC: National Council for the Social Studies.

Fallace, T. (2009). John Dewey's influence on the origins of the social studies: An analysis of the historiography and new interpretation. *Review of Educational Research 79*(2), 601–24.

Fallace, T. D. (2011). *Dewey and the Dilemma of Race: An Intellectual History 1895–1922.* New York: Teachers College Press.

Finch, H. (1942). Reverse chronology: A method in teaching European history. *The Social Studies 33*(8), 364–65.

Finn Jr., C. E. (2003). Foreword. In J. Leming, L. Ellington, & K. Porter (Eds.), *Where Did the Social Studies Go Wrong?* (pp. I–VII). Washington, DC: Thomas B. Fordham Foundation.

Finn Jr., C. E. (2013, September 18). Social studies and poison gas. Retrieved from https://edexcellence.net/social-studies-and-poison-gas

Fonseca-Azevedo, K., & Herculano-Houzel, S. (2012). Metabolic constraint imposes tradeoff between body size and number of brain neurons in human evolution. *Proceedings of the National Academy of Sciences in the United States of America 109*(45), 18571–76.

Fraenkel, J. R. (1981). The relationship between moral thought and moral action: Implications for social studies education. *Theory and Research in Social Education 9*(2), 39–54.

Frazee, B., & Ayers, S. (2003). Garbage in, garbage out: Expanding environments, constructivism, and content knowledge in social studies. In J. Leming, L. Ellington, & K. Porter (Eds.), *Where Did Social Studies Go Wrong?* (pp. 111–23). Washington, DC: Thomas B. Fordham Foundation.

Funk, C., & Rainie, L. (2015). Public and scientists' views on science and society. Retrieved from http://www.pewinternet.org/2015/01/29/public-and-scientists-views-on-science-and-society/

Gay, G. (2002). Preparing for culturally responsive teaching. *Journal of Teacher Education 53*(2), 106–16.

Gay, G. (2010). *Culturally Responsive Teaching: Theory, Research, and Practice* (2nd ed.). New York: Teachers College Press.

Glassman, M. (2001). Dewey and Vygotsky: Society, experience, and inquiry in educational practice. *Educational Researcher 30*(4), 3–14.

Goodlad, J. I. (1984). *A Place Called School: Prospects for the Future*. New York: McGraw-Hill Book Company.

Grant, S. G. (2003). *History Lessons: Teaching, Learning, and Testing in U.S. High School Classrooms*. Mahwah, NJ: Lawrence Erlbaum Associates, Inc.

Grant, S. G., Gradwell, J. M., & Cimbricz, S. K. (2004). A question of authenticity: The document-based question as an assessment of students' knowledge of history. *Journal of Curriculum and Supervision 19*(4), 309–37.

Guidry, A. O. (2008). Character education through a reflective moral inquiry: A revised model that answers old questions. *Journal of Curriculum and Instruction 2*(1), 21–37. doi:10.3776/joci.2008.v2n1p21–37

Hart, L. C. (2002). Preservice teachers' beliefs and practice after participating in an integrated content/methods course. *School Science and Mathematics 102*, 4–14.

Hawley, T. S. (2010). Purpose into practice: The problems and possibilities of rationale-based practice in social studies. *Theory & Research in Social Education 38*(1), 131–62.

Hawley, T. S., & Crowe, A. R. (2016). Making their own path: Preservice teachers' development of purpose in social studies teacher education. *Theory & Research in Social Education 44*(3), 416–47.

Hawley, T. S., Pifel, A. R., & Jordan, A. W. (2012). Structure, citizenship, and professionalism: Exploring rationale development as part of graduate education in social studies. *Journal of Social Studies Research 36*(3), 245–57.

Hess, D. (2002). Discussing controversial public issues in secondary social studies classrooms: Learning from skilled teachers. *Theory and Research in Social Education 30*(1), 10–41.

Hess, D. (2008). Controversial issues and democratic discourse. In L. S. Levstik & C. A. Tyson (Eds.), *Handbook of Research in Social Studies Education* (pp. 124–36). New York: Routledge.

Hess, D. (2010). Discussion in social studies: Is it worth the trouble? In W. C. Parker (Ed.), *Social Studies Today: Research and Practice* (pp. 205–13). New York: Routledge.

Hess, F. M. (2013, September 18). A content-free framework for K-12 social studies. Retrieved from http://www.aei.org/publication/a-content-free-framework-for-k-12-social-studies-standards/

Hickman, L. A. (2001). *Philosophical Tools for Technological Culture: Putting Pragmatism to Work*. Bloomington, IN: Indiana University Press.

Hirsch, E. D. (1988). *Cultural Literacy: What Every American Needs to Know*. New York: Random House.

Hook, S. (2008). *The Metaphysics of Pragmatism*. New York: Cosimo, Inc. 1927.

Hotz, R. L. (2017, April 4). Can handwriting make you smarter? *The Wall Street Journal*. Retrieved from https://www.wsj.com/articles/can-handwriting-make-you-smarter-1459784659

Hunt, M. P., & Metcalf, L. E. (1955). *Teaching High School Social Studies: Problems in Reflective Thinking and Social Understanding*. New York: Harper and Row.

Hursh, D. (1994). Reflective practice and the culture of schools. In E. W. Ross (Ed.), *Reflective Practice in Social Studies* (pp. 69–76). Washington, DC: National Council for the Social Studies.

Ihde, D. (1993). *Philosophy of Technology: An Introduction*. New York: Paragon House.

John Saye & Social Studies Inquiry Research Collaborative (SSIRC). (2013). Authentic pedagogy: Its presence in social studies classrooms and relationship to student performance on state-mandated tests. *Theory & Research in Social Education 41*(1), 89–132.

Jonas, M. E. (2011). Dewey's conception of interest and its significance for teacher education. *Educational Philosophy and Theory 43*(2), 112–29. doi:10.1111/j.1469-5812.2009.00543.x

Kahne, J., & Westheimer, J. (2006). Teaching democracy: What schools need to do. In E. W. Ross (Ed.), *The Social Studies Curriculum: Purposes, Problems, and Possibilities* (pp. 297–316). Albany, NY: State University of New York Press.

Kliebard, H. M. (2006). Dewey's reconstruction of the curriculum: From occupations to disciplined knowledge. In D. T. Hansen (Ed.), *John Dewey and Our Educational Prospect: A Critical Engagement with Dewey's Democracy and Education* (pp. 113–27). Albany, NY: State University of New York Press.

Kraut, R. (2015). Plato. In E. N. Zalta (Ed.), *The Stanford Encyclopedia of Philosophy*. Stanford, CA: Metaphysics Research Lab, Stanford University. Retrieved from http://plato.stanford.edu/archives/spr2015/entries/plato/.

Ladson-Billings, G. (2001). But that's just good teaching! The case for culturally relevant pedagogy. *Theory into Practice 34*(3), 159–65.

Levstik, L. S., & Barton, K. C. (2011). *Doing History: Investigating with Children in Elementary and Middle Schools* (4th ed.). New York: Routledge.

Lieberman, M. (1975). *Evaluation of a Social Studies Curriculum Based on an Inquiry Method and a Cognitive-Developmental Approach to Moral Education.* Paper presented at the Annual Meeting of the American Education Research Association, Washington, DC.

Lortie, D. C. (1975). *Schoolteacher: A Sociological Study.* Chicago, IL: University of Chicago Press.

Lybarger, M. (1983). Origins of the modern social studies: 1900–1916. *History of Education Quarterly 23*(4), 455–68. doi:10.2307/368079

Maslow, A. H. (1987). *Motivation and Personality* (3rd ed.). New York: Harper & Row, Publishers, Inc.

Mason, L. E. (2016). Cultivating civic habits: A Deweyan analysis of the National Council for the Social Studies position statement on guidelines for social studies teaching and learning. *Education and Culture 32*(1), 87–110.

Massialas, B. G. (1992). The "New Social Studies"—Retrospect and prospect. *The Social Studies 83*(3), 120–24.

McGee Banks, C. A., & Banks, J. A. (1995). Equity pedagogy: An essential component of multicultural education. *Theory into Practice 34*(3), 152–58.

Merelman, R. M. (1979). A critique of moral education in the social studies. *Journal of Moral Education 8*(3), 182–92.

Merriam-Webster. (2017). Definition of inquiry. Retrieved from https://www.merriam-webster.com/dictionary/inquiry

Milo, G. (2015). Why do students hate history? *Education Week 35*(5), 19, 21. Retrieved from http://www.edweek.org/ew/articles/2015/09/23/why-do-students-hate-history.html

Misco, T. (2010). Remediation for another high-stakes test: An up-close, personal look inside a remedial test preparation course for a social studies exit exam reveals mastery of simple content—but at what cost? *Kappa Delta Pi Record 46*(3), 121–26.

Misco, T., & Patterson, N. (2009). An old fad of great promise: Reverse chronology history teaching. *Journal of Social Studies Research 33*(1), 71–90.

Misco, T. (2014). Powerful social studies unit design: A companion to powerful social studies teaching and learning. *The Clearing House 87*, 241–48. doi:10.1080/00098655.2014.938598

Misco, T., & Hamot, G. E. (2012). "He was the opposite of what we learned a teacher should be": A study of preservice social studies students' cooperating teachers. *The Journal of Social Studies Research 36*(4), 305–28.

Misco, T., & Shively, J. (2010). Seeing through the forest through the trees: Some renewed thinking on dispositions specific to social studies education. *The Social Studies 101*(3), 121–26.

Mitcham, C. (1994). *Thinking through Technology: The Path between Engineering and Philosophy*. Chicago, IL: University of Chicago Press.

Mitcham, C. (2009). Philosophy of information technology. In C. Hanks (Ed.), *Technology and Values: Essential Readings*. Malden, MA: Wiley-Blackwell.

National Academy of Sciences Institute of Medicine. (2008). *Science, Evolution, and Creationism* (2nd ed.). Washington, DC: National Academy Press.

National Center for Education Statistics. (2015). The Nation's Report Card: 2014 U.S. history, geography, and civics at grade 8. Retrieved from https://nces.ed.gov/pubsearch/pubsinfo.asp?pubid=2015112

National Council for the Social Studies. (2010). *National Curriculum Standards for Social Studies: A Framework for Teaching, Learning and Assessment*. Silver Spring, MD: National Council for the Social Studies.

National Council for the Social Studies. (2013). *College, Career & Civic life (C3) Framework for Social Studies State Standards: Guidance for Enhancing the Rigor of K-12 Civics, Economics, Geography, and History*. Silver Spring, MD: NCSS.

National Council for the Social Studies. (2016). A vision of powerful teaching and learning in the social studies. *Social Education 80*(3), 180–82.

Neill, T. P. (1960). Dewey's ambivalent attitude toward history. In J. Blewett (Ed.), *John Dewey: His Thought and Influence* (pp. 145–60). New York: Fordham University Press.

Nelson, M. R. (1994). The social studies in secondary education: A reprint of the seminal 1916 report with annotations and commentaries (Report No. ISBN-0-941339-20-3). Washington, DC: National Council for the Social Studies. Retrieved from ERIC database. (ED 374072)

Newmann, F. M. (1975). *Education for Citizen Action: Challenge for Secondary Curriculum*. Berkeley, CA: McCutchan.

Newmann, F. M. (1977). Building a rationale for citizenship education. In J. P. Shaver (Ed.), *Building Rationales for Citizenship Education* (pp. 1–31). Washington, DC: National Council for the Social Studies.

Newmann, F. M., Bryk, A. S., & Nagaoka, J. K. (2001). Authentic intellectual work and standardized tests: Conflict or coexistence? Retrieved from http://ccsr.uchicago.edu/publications/p0a02.pdf

Newmann, F. M., & Oliver, D. W. (1970). *Clarifying Public Controversy: An Approach to Social Studies*. Boston, MA: Little, Brown and Company.

Nye, D. E. (2006). *Technology Matters: Questions to Live With*. Cambridge, MA: The MIT Press.

O'Brien, L. M. (2002). A response to "Dewey and Vygotsky: Society, experience, and inquiry in educational practice". *Educational Researcher 31*(5), 21–23.

Ochoa-Becker, A. S. (1996). Building a rationale for issues-centered education. In R. W. Evans & D. W. Saxe (Eds.), *Handbook on Teaching Social Issues. NCSS Bulletin 93* (pp. 6–13). Washington, DC: National Council for the Social Studies.

Ochoa-Becker, A. S. (2007). *Democratic Education for Social Studies: An Issues-Centered Decision Making Curriculum.* Greenwich, CT: Information Age Publishing.

Okan, Z. (2003). Edutainment: Is learning at risk? *British Journal of Educational Technology 34*(3), 255–64.

Pajares, M. F. (1992). Teachers' beliefs and educational research: Cleaning up a messy construct. *Review of Educational Research 62*(3), 307–32.

Pamental, M. (2010). A transactional approach to moral development. *Ethics and Education 5*(1), 15–26. doi:10.1080/17449641003590563

Parker, W. C. (2003). *Teaching Democracy: Unity and Diversity in Public Life*. New York: Teachers College Press.

Pring, R. (2007). *John Dewey: A Philosopher of Education for Our Time?* London: Continuum International Publishing Group.

Quammen, D. (2004). Was Darwin wrong? *National Geographic 206*(5), 2–35.

Richardson, V. (2003). Preservice teachers' beliefs. *Advances in Teacher Education 6*(1), 22.

Rochester, J. M. (2003). The training of idiots: Civics education in America's schools. In J. Leming, L. Ellington, & K. Porter (Eds.), *Where Did Social Studies Go Wrong?* (pp. 6–39). Washington, DC: Thomas B. Fordham Foundation.

Rogers, M. L. (2012). Introduction: Revisiting *The Public and Its Problems*. In J. Dewey & M. L. Rogers (Eds.), *The Public and Its Problems: An Essay in Political Inquiry* (pp. 1–29). University Park, PA: The Pennsylvania State University Press.

Rokeach, M. (1968). *Beliefs, Attitudes, and Values: A Theory of Organization and Change*. San Francisco, CA: Jossey-Bass.

Ross, E. W. (1994). Teachers as curriculum theorizers. In E. W. Ross (Ed.), *Reflective Practice in Social Studies* (pp. 35–41). Washington, DC: National Council for the Social Studies.

Ross, E. W., & Hannay, L. M. (1986). Towards a critical theory of reflective inquiry: Theme. *Journal of Teacher Education 37*(9), 9–15. doi:10.1177/002248718603700402

Rugg, H. O. (1939). Curriculum design in the social sciences: What I believe. In J. A. Michener (Ed.), *The Future of the Social Studies: Proposals for an Experimental Social-Studies Curriculum* (pp. 140–58). Washington, DC: National Council for the Social Studies.

Sadaf, A., Newby, T. J., & Ertmer, P. A. (2012). Exploring pre-service teachers' beliefs about using Web 2.0 technologies in K-12 classroom. *Computers & Education 59*(3), 937–45.

Saxe, W. D. (1992). Framing a theory for social studies foundations. *Review of Educational Research 62*(3), 259–77.

Saye, J. (2013). Authentic pedagogy: Its presence in social studies classrooms and relationship to student performance on state-mandated tests. *Theory and Research in Social Education 41*(1), 89–132. doi:10.1080/00933104.2013.756785.

Scheurman, G., & Newmann, F. M. (1998). Authentic intellectual work in social studies: Putting performance before pedagogy. Retrieved from http://www.learner.org/workshops/socialstudies/pdf/session4/4.AuthInellectualWork.pdf.

Schug, M. C. (1982). *Why Kids Don't Like Social Studies*. Paper presented at the Annual Meeting of the National Council for the Social Studies, Boston, MA. Retrieved from http://files.eric.ed.gov/.

Selznick, P. (1992). *The Moral Commonwealth: Social Theory and the Promise of Community*. Los Angeles, CA: University of California Press.

Shaver, J. P. (1977). Needed: A Deweyan rationale for the social studies. *The High School Journal 60*(8), 345–52.

Shaver, J. P., & Strong, W. (1982). *Facing Value Decisions: Rationale-Building for Teachers*. New York: Teachers College Press.

Sherman, R. R. (1977). The philosophy of John Dewey: Implications for teaching method in the social studies. *The High School Journal 60*(8), 371–78.

Shively, J. M., & VanFossen, P. J. (2009). Toward assessing Internet use in the social studies classroom: Developing an inventory based on a review of relevant literature. *Journal of Social Studies Research 33*(1), 1–32.

Shriner, M., Clark, D. A., Nail, M., Schlee, B. M., & Libler, R. (2010). Social studies instruction: Changing teacher confidence in classrooms enhanced by technology. *The Social Studies 101*, 37–45.

Simon, F. (2002). Moral development: Some suggested implications for the social studies teacher. *The Social Studies LXVI*(4), 150–53.

Smith, J. B., Lee, V. E., & Newmann, F. M. (2001). Instruction and achievement in Chicago elementary schools. Retrieved from http://ccsr.uchicago.edu/publications/p0f01.pdf.

Smith III, J. P., & Girod, M. (2003). John Dewey & psychologizing the subject-matter: Big ideas, ambitious teaching, and teacher education. *Teaching and Teacher Education 19*, 295–307.

Stahl, R. J. (1979). Developing values dilemmas for content-centered social studies instruction; theoretical construct and practical applications. *Theory and Research in Social Education VII*(2), 50–75.

Stanley, W. B. (2010). Social studies and the social order. In W. C. Parker (Ed.), *Social Studies Today: Research and Practice* (pp. 17–24). New York: Routledge.

Stanley, W. O., & Stanley III, W. O. (1977). Dewey: The role of social studies in education. *The High School Journal 60*(8), 365–70.

Stuckart, D. W. (2014). Philosophical guidelines for the social studies: Enhancing intelligence with digital tools and artifacts. In D. J. Loveless, B. Griffith, M. E. Berci, E. Ortlieb, & P. M. Sullivan (Eds.), *Academic Knowledge Construction and Multimodal Curriculum Development* (pp. 53–70). Hershey, PA: IGI Global.

Stuckart, D. W., & Glanz, J. (2010). *Revisiting Dewey: Best Practices for Educating the Whole Child Today*. Lanham, MD: Rowman & Littlefield Education.

Swan, K., & Hicks, D. (2006). Through the democratic lens: The role of purpose in leveraging technology to support historical inquiry in the social studies classroom. *International Journal of Social Education 21*(2), 142–68.

Taba, H. (1963). Learning by discovery: Psychological and educational rationale. *The Elementary School Journal 63*(6), 308–316.

Taba, H. (1967). *Teacher's Handbook for Elementary Social Studies*. Palo Alto, CA: Addison-Wesley.

Tannebaum, R. P. (2013). Dialogue, discussion, and democracy in the social studies classroom. *Social Studies Research and Practice 8*(3), 99–109.

Tanner, L. N. (1997). *Dewey's Laboratory School: Lessons for Today*. New York: Teachers College Press.

Thornton, S. J. (1994). Perspectives on reflective practice in social studies education. In E. W. Ross (Ed.), *Reflective Practice in Social Studies* (pp. 5–12). Washington, DC: National Council for the Social Studies.

Thornton, S. J. (2005). *Teaching Social Studies That Matters: Curriculum for Active Learning*. New York: Teachers College Press.

Tyack, D. B. (1974). *The One Best System: A History of American Urban Education*. Cambridge, MA: Harvard University Press.

van Inwagen, P., & Sullivan, M. (2015). Metaphysics. *The Stanford Encyclopedia of Philosophy*. Retrieved from http://plato.stanford.edu/archives/spr2015/entries/metaphysics.

VanFossen, P. J., & Waterson, R. A. (2008). "It is just easier to do what you did before . . .": An update on internet use in secondary social studies classrooms in Indiana. *Theory and Research in Social Education 36*(2), 124–52.

Vinson, K. D. (1999). National curriculum standards and social studies education: Dewey, Freire, Foucalt, and the construction of radical critique. *Theory and Research in Social Education 27*(3), 296–328.

Wade, R. (2002). Beyond expanding horizons: New curriculum directions for elementary social studies. *The Elementary School Journal 103*(115–30).

Washington, E. Y., & Humphries, E. K. (2011). A social studies teacher's sense making of controversial issues discussions of race in a predominantly white, rural high school classroom. *Theory and Research in Social Education 39*(1), 92–114.

Westbrook, R. B. (1991). *John Dewey and American Democracy*. Ithaca, NY: Cornell University Press.

Wheeler, J. E. (1977). John Dewey's philosophy as a blueprint for the future. *The High School Journal 60*(8), 387–94.

Whitworth, S., & Berson, M. J. (2002). Computer technology in the social studies: An examination of the effectiveness. *Contemporary Issues in Technology and Teacher Education 2*(4), 471–508.

Williams, J. P. (2014, February 27). Who is fighting against Common Core? *U.S. News & World Report*. Retrieved from https://www.usnews.com/news/special-reports/a-guide-to-common-core/articles/2014/02/27/who-is-fighting-against-common-core.

Wineburg, S. (2001). *Historical Thinking and Other Unnatural Acts: Charting the Future of Teaching the Past*. Philadelphia, PA: Temple University Press.

Wraga, W. G. (1999). Organizing and developing issues-centered social studies curricula: Profiting from our predecessor. *The Social Studies 90*(5), 209–217.

Wronski, S. P. (1993). Persistent issues in the social studies. In V. S. Wilson, J. A. Litle, & G. L. Wilson (Eds.), *Teaching Social Studies: Handbook of Trends, Issues, and Implications for the Future* (pp. 5–23). Westport, CT: Greenwood Press.

Index

active occupations, 20, 28, 30, 41, 43–45, 46, 62
aims, 6, 10, 20, 21, 28, 29, 36–38, 40, 41, 43, 48, 49, 63, 68, 69, 78, 99, 102, 107, 121
appraisal and appraising, 80–81, 86
Aristotle, 14–16
associated living, 12, 25, 29, 87, 92, 94, 97, 109, 111, 113
authentic intellectual work (AIW), 44–46

beliefs, general, 2, 15, 20, 22–24, 49, 53–54, 56–59, 70–71, 82, 89, 94, 105, 112, 116, 118, 120–21; teacher, 27–29, 34–38, 46–47, 51, 117
big ideas, 47
Bruner, Jerome, 39, 83

character, 1, 3, 38, 66, 71, 73, 83, 85–87, 89
citizenship, xv, 1, 3, 10, 22–26, 36–37, 39, 85, 91, 106, 107–8, 110, 115–16, 118
Citizenship Transmission, 28, 38–40, 86, 121
Common Core State Standards (CCSS), 20, 40, 90–91, 99, 103, 107, 116

consequences in thinking, 1, 3, 13, 17, 18, 25–26, 33, 47–48, 50, 57, 59, 62, 68, 72–74, 79–81, 85–87, 90–92, 94, 97, 104–5, 107, 109–11, 113, 121
contextualism, 82, 84
controversial public issues (CPI), 3, 41, 87, 91, 99–100, 115–18
culturally relevant, responsive pedagogy, 63
curriculum gatekeeper, 36–37, 48, 105–6

Darwin, Charles, 4, 7, 12, 54, 56, 58, 90, 98
democracy, xii, xv, xvi, 1–3, 8, 10–14, 18, 21–26, 50, 52–53, 58–59, 63, 68, 82, 85, 108, 112–18, 120–22
denotative method, 53, 56, 58–59, 62
desire, 54–55, 60–61, 70, 72, 74, 78–81, 86–87, 92, 105, 108
Dewey, misunderstood, xvi, 6, 8, 11, 16, 20, 26, 61, 92
Dewey's critics, 37, 62, 68–69, 98, 104
discussion in the classroom, 3, 41–42, 44, 49, 88, 91, 99–100, 105, 107, 115, 118–19, 122

diversity, 23, 25, 33–34, 42, 44, 63–64, 85–88, 101, 108, 110–11, 114, 118–21
dogmatism, 11, 38, 58, 85
dualisms, xvi, 14–16, 20, 31, 33, 49, 54, 60–61, 86, 91, 93

effort, 1, 27, 71–73, 75, 78–79, 89
end-in-view, 33, 37, 55, 72, 74, 79, 81, 86
English, 27, 50
epistemology, 14–15, 36, 90–91
ethics, 1–2, 13, 25, 60, 68, 71–72, 79, 81–82, 88, 114
event, 9, 18, 32, 46–48, 50–51, 56, 65–69, 96, 100, 104–5, 111, 120; defined, 66
evolution, 4–6, 9, 12–14, 17, 19, 24, 28–31, 33, 54, 56–58, 70, 79, 91, 93, 96, 98, 108, 111, 121
experience, 1–3, 6, 8, 12–14, 17, 18–21, 23, 25–35, 37, 41–44, 47–57, 59–71, 73–76, 78–79, 82, 86–88, 90–92, 94, 97–100, 102, 105, 108, 113, 115–16, 118–21; continuity of, xvii; educative, 53–54, 59–61, 74, 102; mis-educative, 54, 102; primary, 31, 50, 55–56, 62–64, 73, 76, 96, 98; secondary, 55–56, 62–64, 70, 79
an experience, xvi, 13

Fallace, Thomas, 6, 11–12, 22
Freire, Paolo, 83

geography, 6, 11, 17–20, 27–28, 34, 37, 39, 43, 48, 50–54, 90, 98–99, 102, 104
Greeks, ancient, xvi, 14–16, 82, 97
government, 12, 17, 50, 104, 111–12

habit, xii, 13, 24–25, 29, 49–50, 54–56, 65–66, 71–73, 78, 80, 84–87, 95, 97, 101, 105, 108, 111

Hegel, Friedrich, 16
Hickman, Larry, 55, 93, 95
history, xv–xvii, 1–2, 6–7, 10–11, 13–14, 17–20, 24–26, 28–29, 34, 37, 39–40, 42–43, 46–48, 50–55, 57–58, 61–63, 67–70, 76, 82, 90, 94, 95, 97–100, 102, 104, 111, 115–17

Idealists, 16
imagination, 81, 93, 96
impulses, 37, 56, 72–76, 78, 84–87
inclusion, 25, 45, 63, 83, 85–86, 121
indoctrination, 11, 24–25, 38, 51, 85, 87, 117
Industrial Revolution, industrialization, xii, 6–7, 72, 96
inference, 67
inquiry, xv–xvi, 2–3, 6, 9, 11–12, 14–15, 18–19, 24–26, 28, 32, 35, 38–42, 44–48, 50–51, 56, 61–62, 64, 66, 77, 80, 85, 87, 89–101, 102–6, 110, 113–14, 116
instrumental, instrumentalism, 1, 3, 5–6, 13, 19, 21, 25, 48, 52–53, 55–56, 60, 64, 68–69, 71, 73, 79–81, 83, 86, 90, 92–93, 95–99, 102, 105, 109, 112–13, 121
intelligence, intelligent activity, 2, 10, 13–14, 17, 21–28, 31–32, 48, 51, 53–54, 58–59, 64, 70, 72–74, 78, 81, 84–85, 90–92, 94–95, 102–3, 105, 108–9, 111, 121
intelligent design theory, 56–57
interest, xv, xvii, 1, 3, 14–15, 18–22, 24–26, 28, 34, 37, 40–44, 48–50, 55, 59–61, 63, 68–81, 83, 88–89, 100–103, 108, 110–13, 118–21
issues-centered lessons, 2, 42, 44, 47, 115, 117

judgment, 2, 12, 25, 35, 44, 52–53, 64–68, 70–73, 75, 78–81, 83–84, 86, 88, 92, 100, 109, 114, 120–21

Kapp, Ernst, 101
knowledge, xv–xvii, 6, 13, 16, 20–23, 25, 27, 30–36, 38, 41–44, 46–48, 52–53, 55, 58, 62–63, 90–95, 99–100, 104–5, 118; disciplinary, xv, 20, 23, 28, 32, 34, 43, 46, 69; prior, 46, 50, 70, 99–100; theory of, 20
Kohlberg, Lawrence, 83–84

Laboratory School, 8–9, 43, 87
language, 27, 29, 36, 48, 50–51, 94, 98, 117
long-term projects, 2, 42, 44, 46–47

Marx, Karl, 7, 101
Marxism, 5
Maslow's hierarchy, 75
math and mathematics, 27–28, 31, 34, 36, 48, 50–52, 55, 96, 98
metaphysics, 8, 12, 14–17, 31, 33
middle position, xvii, 6, 17, 20–21, 33, 40, 43, 84, 99
Misco, Thomas, 12, 22, 34, 41, 44, 46–47
morality, morals, 1–3, 13, 26, 47, 53, 60, 64–66, 71–73, 81–89, 108, 110, 121
moral theory, 81–82, 84, 110
moral values, 66, 81
motivation, 36, 74–76, 78
multicultural education, 63–64

National Council for the Social Studies (NCSS), xvi, 22, 37, 47, 91, 106–7
natural selection, 12, 29, 58, 90

object, 15–17, 19, 27, 30, 32–33, 36, 50, 52, 56–57, 70, 73–81, 91, 96–97, 103, 105, 108, 110
ontology, 14–15, 18–20, 65, 90–92, 94, 97

phenomenology, 101
physis, 15, 79

Plato, 16, 19
play, 43, 74
pleasure, 55, 69, 75–78
pluralism, plurality, 22, 63, 85, 86, 87, 108, 110, 112, 116, 118, 120–21
positivism, 5, 101
pragmatism, pragmatists, 1, 5–7, 13, 31, 42, 49, 54–55, 69, 83, 93, 95, 97, 101, 105
psychologizing the curriculum, 27–28, 32, 48–49, 61–62
psychology, 7–8, 15, 18, 31, 34, 41, 43, 73–75
publics, 24, 107–14, 118

realists, 16
reason, 17, 32, 54
reflective inquiry activity, 35, 66, 100
Reflective Inquiry teachers, 25, 28, 38–41, 48
reverse chronology units, 2, 42, 44, 46–47

schools, purpose of, xii, 2, 10, 13–14, 19, 21–22, 25, 61, 72, 96, 101–2, 119, 121
science, 12, 14–15, 30–31, 45, 48, 50–52, 56–59, 61–62, 82, 84, 89, 93–98, 101, 107
situation, 2, 13, 24–25, 33, 41, 51, 54–56, 60–62, 64–67, 69, 71, 73, 75, 77–80, 82, 88, 90, 92–98, 103, 108–9, 112, 114
social sciences, xi–xiii, 6, 11, 17–20, 23, 25–26, 28, 34, 37, 39–40, 51, 72, 84, 86, 110, 116
Social Scientist teachers, 28, 36, 38–40
stasis, 17
the state, 109, 111–14, 121

teacher rationale, xi, 2–3, 7, 22–26, 116
techne, 15, 79, 100–101
technology, 26, 36, 82, 91–92, 100–103, 105

thematic units, 2, 44, 46, 49, 116
thinking, 14–15, 20, 25, 29, 32–33, 35, 42, 46, 50–55, 62, 67, 70, 73, 75–76, 78, 82, 85–86, 89, 92, 95–100, 102–5, 107, 110, 113, 121
Thornton, Stephen, 12, 18, 34, 36–37, 41, 48
tools, 1, 13–14, 20, 25, 32, 39, 42–43, 49, 67–68, 70, 85, 90, 91, 93, 95–96, 99–106, 110–11, 117, 120

valuation theory, 71, 80
values, 3, 7, 21, 23–24, 36, 38, 59, 65–66, 69, 70, 78, 83–86, 115–18, 121
valuing, 64, 68, 79–81, 86–87
a vision for social studies teachers, xii, 1–3, 5–7, 21–22, 24, 26–28, 45, 51, 63–64, 73, 91, 108, 120, 122

warranted assertability, 94
Westbrook, Robert, 8, 14, 108, 112, 114

About the Author

Daniel W. Stuckart is an associate professor at the City University of New York Lehman College in the Bronx, New York City. He serves as the undergraduate middle and high school education adviser, coordinator for the graduate Social Studies Education Program, and faculty director of the New York City Teaching Fellows Program. He has also been an officer with the New York State Association of Teacher Educators since 2012. His research interests include the intersection of philosophy, urban education, and democratic practices.

Dr. Stuckart has published extensively about democratic teaching and learning in the social studies, including the use of technology. He has presented his work at numerous regional, state, national, and international conferences. He is also coauthor of a book entitled, *Revisiting Dewey: Best Practices for Educating the Whole Child Today* (2010).

www.ingramcontent.com/pod-product-compliance
Lightning Source LLC
Chambersburg PA
CBHW031553300426
44111CB00006BA/299